AF429296

THE

HBCU

EXPERIENCE

AMERICA'S FIRST BLACK REALITY TV SERIES EDITION

Celebrating 20 Years

Visionary Author: Dr. Ashley Little
Lead Author: Ray Cunningham
Celebrity Foreword Author: Ray J

Copyright @ 2023 by The HBCU Experience Movement, LLC

All rights reserved. No portion of this book may be reproduced, stored in a retrieval system, or transmitted by any means electronic, mechanical, photocopy recording, scanning, or other except brief quotations without prior written permission of the publisher, except in case of brief quotations embodied in critical reviews and certain other noncommercial uses permitted by copyright law.

For permission requests, write to the publisher, addressed|

"Attention Permissions Coordinator," at
thehbcuexperiencemovement@gmail.com

Published By: The HBCU Experience Movement, LLC

The HBCU Experience Movement, LLC

thehbcuexperiencemovement@gmail.com

Ordering Information:
Quantity Sales: Special discounts are available on quantity purchases by corporations, associations, and nonprofits. For details, contact the publisher at the address above.

ISBN: 979-8-218-21921-5

DR. ASHLEY LITTLE

A Message from the Founder
Dr. Ashley Little

Historically Black Colleges & Universities (HBCUs) were established to serve the educational needs of black Americans. During the time of their establishment, and many years afterward, blacks were generally denied admission to traditionally white institutions. Prior to The Civil War, there was no structured higher education system for black students. Public policy, and certain statutory provisions, prohibited the education of blacks in various parts of the nation. Today, HBCUs represent a vital component of American higher education.

The HBCU Experience Movement, LLC is a collection of stories from prominent alumni throughout the world, who share how their HBCU experience molded them into the people they are today. We are also investing financially into HBCUs throughout the country. Our goal is to create a global movement of prominent HBCU alumni throughout the nation to continue to share their stories each year, allowing us to give back to prestigious HBCUs annually.

We are proud to present to you *The HBCU Experience: America's First Black Reality TV Series Edition*. We would like to acknowledge and give a special thanks to our amazing lead author/partner, Ray Cunningham, for your dedication and commitment. We appreciate you and thank you for your hard work and dedication on behalf of this project. We would also like to give a special thanks to our foreword author, contributing authors and partners for believing in this movement and investing your time, and monetary donations, to give back. We appreciate all of the prominent alumni from the series who shared your HBCU experience in this publication.

About Dr. Ashley Little

Dr. Ashley Little is Ms. Georgia Global Continental 2023 and the CEO/Founder of Ashley Little Enterprises, LLC, which encompasses her media, consulting work, writing, ghost writing, book publishing, book coaching, project management, magazine, public relations & marketing, and empowerment speaking. In addition, she is an award-winning serial entrepreneur, TV/radio host, TEDx speaker, international speaker, keynote speaker, media maven, journalist, writer, host, philanthropist, business coach, investor, advisor for She Wins Society, and 21-times award-winning bestselling author. As seen on Black Enterprise (2X), *Forbes* (2X), *Sheen Magazine* (Print and Online), Sheen Talk, Voyage ATL, Fox Soul TV, NBC, Fox, CBS, BlackNews.Com, Shoutout Miami, Shoutout Atlanta, Morning Star, Yahoo Finance, Heart and Soul, The Book of Sean, *HBCU Times, VIP Global Magazine*, The Black Report, Vocal, Ted.com, Medium, Soul Wealth, Hustle and Soul, BlackBusiness.com, Glambitious Top 21 Women Of 2021, New York Weekly's Top 10 Hardest Working CEOs alongside billionaire Mark Cuban, *US Insider's* Top 10 Women Entrepreneurs alongside billionaire and media mogul, Oprah Winfrey, *London Daily Post, Sheen Magazine* 5 Pioneers Making a Difference in Their Communities, NCA&T *Alumni Times*, CEO Weekly Top 10 Influential People in 2021 alongside billionaires Jeff Bezos and Beyonce' and many more. Through the Biden & Harris Administration, and Leaders Esteem Christian Bible University, she was also awarded with the Presidential Lifetime Achievement Award the highest award in the country. She is the Chancellor for Leaders Esteem Christian Bible University(Atlanta campus), and board member as well. Charter member for Dr. Judy Rashid Leadership and Education Center in South Africa.

As a recipient of the "Author of The Year" award by Glambitious, she is also a part of The Forbes Next 1000 Class of 2021 in partnership with Square. This first-of-its-kind initiative celebrates bold and inspiring entrepreneurs who are redefining what it means to run a business. Furthermore, she was a recipient of Nashville's Black 40 Under 40 Awards in December 2021. It is an annual event honoring the best and the brightest for their accomplishments in their chosen field and for their contributions and commitment to the African American community. Dr. Little is also an official member of For(bes) The Culture. For(bes) The Culture was formed in Boston at the Forbes Under 30 Summit in October of 2017. They pride themselves on convening current and future black and brown leaders worldwide to network, collaborate, share opportunities, and discuss issues related to their communities and the planet at-large. She was recognized along with other influential leaders and distinguished entrepreneurs, including Oprah Winfrey, Mel Robbins, Gary V and many more for the annual Brainz 500 Global Awards List awarded by *Brainz Magazine*. Lastly, she is a proud member of The Chancellor's Round Table at North Carolina A&T State University and 2022 Recipient of the Dr. Velma Speight Young Alumna Award at North Carolina A&T State University.

She is a proud member of Delta Sigma Theta Sorority, Incorporated, and a member of Alpha Phi Omega. She is very involved in her community, organizations and non-profits. Currently, she is the co-founder of Sweetheart Scholars non-profit organization, along with three other powerful women. This scholarship is given out annually to African American females from her hometown of Wadesboro, North Carolina who are attending college to help with their expenses. Dr. Little believes it takes a village to raise a child and she also encourages others to never forget where you come from. Dr. Little is a strong believer in giving back to her community. She believes our young ladies need vision, direction and strong mentorship. She is the CEO/Founder/Visionary Author of The HBCU Experience Movement, LLC, the first Black-owned company to launch books written and published by prominent alumni throughout the world who attended Historically Black Colleges & Universities (HBCUs). As authors, they share a powerful collection of stories on how their unique college experience has molded them into the people they are today. The purpose of The HBCU Experience Movement is to change the narrative by sharing Black stories and investing financially back into our HBCUs to increase young alumni giving and enrollment. The award-winning bestselling authors won the Black Authors Matter TV Award in May of 2021, Inaugural Anthem Awards of 2022, as well as the International Book Awards by The American Book Fest. The books are also part of the WorldCat.org, the world's largest network of library content and services. Dr. Little is also the Editor and Chief of *Creating Your Seat at The Table International Magazine*, advisor for She Wins Society, and writing and publishing coach for the WILDE Winner's Circle.

She is the founder and owner of T.A.L.K. Radio & TV Network, LLC, which airs in over 167 countries, and streams live on Facebook, YouTube, Twitter and Periscope. This broadcasting and media production company is for new or existing radio shows, television shows, or other electronic media outlets to air content from a centralized source. All news, information or music shared on this platform are solely the responsibility of the station/radio owner. She is also the owner and creator of Creative Broadcasting Radio Station, the station of "unlimited possibilities." She is also one of the hosts of the new TV Show *Daytime Drama* nationally syndicated television show, which will be aired on Comcast Channel 19 and AT&T Channel 99 in 19 middle Tennessee counties. It will also air on The United Broadcasting Network, The Damascus Roads Broadcasting Network, and Roku.

Dr. Little is a 21X award-winning bestselling author of, *Dear Fear, Volume 2: 18 Powerful Lessons of Living Your Best Life Outside of Fear; The Gyrlfriend Code, Volume 1; I Survived; Girl, Get Up and Win; Glambitious Guide to Being an Entrepreneur; The*

Price of Greatness; The Making of a Successful Business Woman; and *Hello, Queen.* She is a co-host for The Tamie Collins Markee Radio Show, award-winning entrepreneur who is also a reflection contributor for the book, NC Girls Living in a Maryland World, Sales/Marketing/Contributing Writer/Event Correspondent for *SwagHer Magazine,* contributing writer for MizCEO Magazine, contributing editor for *SheIs Magazine,* contributing writer/national sales executive for *Courageous Woman Magazine,* contributing writer for Upwords International Magazine (India), and contributing writer/global partner for Powerhouse Global International Magazine (London). Host of "Creating Your Seat At The Table", Host of "Authors On The Rise", Co-Host Glambitious Podcast, Partner/Visionary Author of The Gyrlfriend Code The Sorority Edition along with The Gyrlfriend Collective, LLC. Lastly, she has received awards, such as "Author of the Month"; The Executive Citation of Anne Arundel County, Maryland Award, which was awarded by the County Executive Steuart L. Pittman; and Top 28 Influential Business Pioneers for *K.I.S.H. Magazine* Spring 2019 Edition. She has been featured in *All About Inspire Magazine, Formidable Magazine, BRAG Magazine,* the front cover of MizCEO Magazine in November of 2019, the front cover for Upwords Magazine in the October 2019 Edition, *Courageous Woman* Special Speakers Edition in November 2019 and *Influence Magazine.* She has been featured on a nationally syndicated television show, *HBCU 101,* on Aspire TV, Dynasty of Dreamers *K.I.S.H. Magazine* Spring 2019 Edition, the front cover of *Courageous Magazine* in December of 2019, the front cover of Doz International Magazine in January 2020, Top 28 Influential Business Pioneers for K.I.S.H. Magazine, *Power20 Magazine Glambitious* January 2020 and *Power20 Magazine Glambitious* February 2020. She was also featured in *Powerhouse Global International London Magazine* March 2020 edition, *National Boss Magazine* in the October 2020 edition, *Sheen Magazine* February 2020 edition as one of "The Top 20 Women to Be on The Lookout for in 2020", BlackNews.com, BlackBusiness.com, the front cover of *She Speaks Magazine* August

2020 edition, as well as the front cover of *National Boss Magazine* November 2020 edition.

In addition, she's been featured on BlackNewsScoop.com, awarded the National Women's Empowerment Ministry "Young, Gifted & Black Award" in February 2020, which honors and celebrates women in business below age 40 for their creativity and business development. Featured in *National Women Empowerment Magazine, Black Enterprise,* as well as on Fox, NBC, and CBS, she was interviewed on *The Black Report* on Fox Soul TV and the front cover for *National Boss Magazine.* She was also a speaker at The Black College Expo 2020, for Creative CEOs Summit in January of 2021, and international speaker for Living Your Dream Life Summit 2021. She was also the speaker for the Elite Business Women Powershift Conference 2021, The Bella, The Brand & Her Bag Wealth Summit 2021, The Unstoppable You Summit in January 2021, the Marketing Mastery Summit for Glambitious 2021, the Crown Yourself Conference in January 2021, as well as the Door Dash Virtual Black History Month Celebration. As the speaker for Day of Aggie Generations with North Carolina A&T State University, Dr. Little was the 2021 Woman of Black Excellence Honoree, guest speaker on the podcast, The Happy Hour Show, speaker for the Phoenix Jack & Jill HBCU Author Showcase, as well as a guest on The JMosley Show. As contributing author for *Prayers for The Entrepreneurial Woman* book, she has spoken at Creative Con, been recognized as one of Today's Black History Makers, as well as being a featured speaker at From Paper to Profits Conference. She has been afforded the opportunity to gain press access for "Don't Waste Your Petty" movie as well as Mahalia Jackson's movie. She's been a speaker for HerStory Women's Global Empowerment Summit, HerStory Women Who Lead Conference, Stepping N2 Sisterhood Sharing Winning Secrets Virtual Summit, I AM Glambitious Virtual Conference, Black Authors Matter TV show, Thought Leaders Global Virtual Summit, as well as A Conversation with Floyd Marshall, Jr. As a Black Authors Matter TV award winner, Grind Pretty Magazine, Revolt. She has spoken for Sheen Talk and served as the foreword author for the anthology *It Cost to Be the Boss*. Recognized by *VIP Global Magazine* as one of the Top 50 Most Influential Women, she has spoken at Black Writers Weekend, The GameChangers with Angela Ward Show, and served as keynote speaker for Blacks in Nonprofits Conference. Having served as speaker for the Leap Conference, Pass the Mic Sis, the From Purpose to Profit Summit, and The Been Worthy Podcast, she has been the speaker and host for The MizCEO graduation, was featured in *Emoir Magazine* for Building a Global Media Empire, Front Cover GlamCEO Magazine December 2022 and was a Making Black History Today recipient for Glambitious, 2023 Woman To Watch for Glambitious, 20 Black Women Entrepreneurs To Watch for BlkWomenHustle, Guest/Speaker on Glambitious Inaugural Live Talk Show Series, Model for Black Beauty Expo 2023, Recipient of The Champion Of Change Award from Colour Me Social Foundation, Black Women Making History for BlkWomenHustle, Speaker/Honoree at The Stepping N2 Sisterhood Conference 2023.

Dr. Little received her undergraduate degree in English from North Carolina A&T State University. She received her master's degree in Leadership and Coaching and her Doctorate in Leadership, as well. Dr. Little is a mover and shaker, and she continuously pushes herself to be better than she was yesterday. She gives God all the credit for everything that has happened in her life. She has strong faith and determination to be great. She believes her only competition is herself. Her favorite scripture is Philippians 4:13: "I can do all things through Christ who strengthens me."

Table of Contents

continued...

RAY J
Ray J from Celebrity Edition 1 & 2

Celebrity Foreword
Ray J
Celebrity Edition Season 1 & 2

It's often said that you're "never too old" to go to college. That message applies to celebrities also! Media mogul Ray J, best known from VH1's *Love and Hip-Hop Hollywood*, was the featured guest speaker for Philander Smith College's popular "Bless the Mic" lecture series during their homecoming festivities in 2018. The HBCU is well known for being affiliated with the United Methodist Church and is a founding member of the United Negro College Fund. After a well-received talk to an audience of more than five hundred students, he spent the next couple of days on campus, enjoying a dose of the Philander Experience. These inspiring encounters led Ray J to decide to enroll at Philander Smith College, a private HBCU located in Little Rock, Arkansas. Ray J's HBCU journey started in the spring semester of 2019 at Philander Smith and continues today as a cast member on both seasons of *College Hill: Celebrity Edition* filmed at Texas Southern University and Alabama State University for BET.

Professionally known as Ray J, William Ray Norwood, Jr. is an American singer, actor and television personality. Born in McComb, Mississippi, and raised in Carson, California, he is the younger brother of legendary singer/actress Brandy and the first cousin of west coast icon Snoop Dogg. The multi-talented star started his career in 1989 when he booked his first commercial at eight years old. Then, he signed with Elektra Records in 1995. He has gone on to attain massive success with several albums, hit singles *Wait a Minute* and *One Wish*, merchandise, and shows under his belt. Ray J played the foster son on *The Sinbad Show* from 1993 to 1994, starring alongside famed comedian Sinbad. When his sister Brandy starred in the hit TV sitcom *Moesha*, he was given the role of Dorian, a.k.a. D-Money, whom he played from 1999 to 2001 on UPN. Ray J went on to land his own dating series on VH1 titled *For the Love of Ray J* and a second VH1 series, *Brandy & Ray J: A Family Business*. He appeared on the UK version of *Celebrity Big Brother* and hosted Oxygen's *Bad Girls All-Star Battle* and WEtv's *Driven to Love*.

As the founder of Raytroniks, Ray J introduced a line of consumer electronics to the United States market. The product categories included electric bikes, smartphone fans, and smartwatches. In particular, the Scoot-E-Bike brand, which Ray J developed, grew exponentially after implementing a viral organic marketing strategy. Ray J secured product placements through celebrities such as Sean Combs, Brandy, Snoop Dogg, Chris Brown and Steph Curry, as well as professional athletic teams, including the L.A. Clippers and the Los Angeles Rams. In November 2017, Ray J co-founded the direct-to-consumer electronics brand called Raycon, which sells wireless audio products such as earbuds and headphones, with him overseeing the brand and strategy. From TV to music and tech, Ray J has done it all. In 2016, he got married to his *Love & Hip Hop Hollywood* co-star, Princess Love. They have two beautiful children, Melody and Epic. Although he's had several publicized controversies, they only seemed to increase his fame. His talent is undeniable, and his drive is commendable.

The entertainment mogul and father of two understands the importance of education, especially that of an HBCU. "God is working! I'm remarkably familiar with the HBCU experience because my parents attended HBCUs," he wrote via his Instagram announcement. "I welcome the opportunity to further my business skills as I continue to grow and expand my technology company Raycon."

Ray J says of HBCUs and the *College Hill* experience, "I do TV and music. Everybody sees me as the turn up guy. But, in real life, I founded a technology company called Raycon Global, and I've had a lot of successes in my career. My mama went to Southern University and my dad went to Jackson State University. So, it's always been in the family. I took this journey on *College Hill* because I want to make my family proud, and I feel like I'm gonna be at the top of my class! No matter what I did last night, I'm gonna be up all night, working! Not only is this show about the culture, but it's the right thing to do to tap in and make sure we support our community!"

RAY CUNNINGHAM
Misster Ray from Season 3

We Are Black History
Ray Cunningham
Season 3

Almost twenty years later, who would have thought *College Hill* would *still* be a topic of conversation amongst the HBCU community? We did! To be eighteen to twenty-one years old, on BET, and graduating college wasn't the normal narrative for young, Black adults in America at the time. But most of us knew something greater would come from this once-in-a-lifetime opportunity. What was regular everyday college life and conversation for us became monumental TV moments that discussed cultural awareness, diversity, equality, community advocacy and self-esteem. We were young, fresh and something new with a historical backdrop—our schools (Southern University, Langston University, Virginia State University, and the University of the Virgin Islands) and respective cities (Chicago, Atlanta and South Beach).

There's not a day that goes by that a "bring back *College Hill*" tweet isn't tweeted to BET, along with the million-dollar question: When is BET bringing back the alumni for a reunion show? As adults, the *College Hill* family is just that: a *family*. You see, some don't speak, and some have become remarkably close. But what bonds us all over time is the show. Our separate show experiences played a part in our lives and careers. We really showed our age when we got together during the pandemic in 2020 for our viral Instagram challenge.

Our nostalgic TV moments of roommates camping in the woods, disagreeing over ribs, hot tub shenanigans, and twirling heels have become viral MEMES and GIFs on social media. No shock to us, *College Hill* was the most streamed series in 2020 during the pandemic on the newly launched BET+ app, which let executives know that the audience wanted that old thang back! In the TV era of reboots, BET and Edmonds Entertainment relaunched *College Hill*, but with a twist: celebrities who were pursuing higher education at HBCUs! We admit, *Celebrity Edition* wasn't on anyone's bingo card for 2022. But close to one million fans tuned into the premiere, starring Ray J, Stacey Dash, Big Freedia, Lamar Odom, India Love, Dreamdoll, Slim Thug and Nene Leakes! For better or worse, these wild and hilarious moments on *College Hill* captivated audiences, leaving them to savor the first moments of unscripted Black college life on TV.

With greatness comes the need for receipts. Here's some answers from some questions the fans have been asking over the years:

Q: Do I share cognac now?
A: YES! I'm a tequila guy these days!

Q: Did Krystal and Vanessa ever make up after Season 4?
A: YES! They broke the internet in 2022 when The Shade Room posted a picture of them together hanging out in Florida!

Q: Did the celebrities actually go to class on *Celebrity Edition*?
A: YES! I met their teachers when I hosted an event for one of their class projects.

Q: Why are Seasons 1 and 2 locked away in the BET vault and not available for streaming anywhere?
A: That's above my pay grade!

We were not only the *first* Black reality stars, but we were also our own managers, stylists who had to dress ourselves from our own closets for scenes and photoshoots on a college budget. We were our own hairstylists, barbers, make-up artists, travel agents and publicists! Before there were blog headlines, you had to go to our MySpace Top 8 to see who was not getting along. That was the original social media! We were living our best lives, hitting the red carpets at the BET Awards, BET Hip Hop Awards, Rip the Runway,

Spring Bling, Celebration of Gospel and getting to be guests on 106 & PARK. Just imagine being in college and regularly being in the room as a celebrity guest with actual celebrities we were fans of at the time!

America couldn't get enough of *College Hill*. Cast members appeared in *KING Magazine*, hosted *Rap City in the Basement*, launched successful brands, appeared in numerous TV sitcoms, including *IN THE CUT*, were in commercials for Subway and films like *Meet The Spartans*, *The Assistant* and *Stalker*, to appearing on other reality shows, such as: *Bad Girls Club: Bad Girls Need Love Too, Love & Hip Hop Hollywood, The Real Housewives of Dubai* and *My Flipping Family*. The most amazing part of *College Hill* is the number of students we influenced to attend HBCUs back then who come up to us now with their children to thank us for the show and to tell us how it played a part in pursing their higher education. Fans acknowledge the historical context of the show and have seen us grow up through social media. How cool is it to say that Grammy-winning R&B legend Kenneth "Babyface" Edmonds was your show's executive producer, then to have legendary rappers Ludacris and Trina doing voice-overs for your season? The show gave us some unique, once-in-a-lifetime moments, including going to civil rights icon Rosa Parks' funeral in Washington D.C. during Season 3 and traveling internationally to London during Season 5.

As the twentieth anniversary approaches, none of us entering the house knew that once we had gotten to an age when going to the club isn't that fun anymore, bedtime is at 9 p.m., work calls before friends do, and our parents are now our best friends, that people would *still* be giving us the "you look familiar" face in public. Considering that the majority of the former housemates are now married with normal lives, I can only imagine that being an interesting conversation of clarification on the ride home for some!

From the DVD releases, digital clips on social media for throwback Thursday posts and streaming on platforms such as BET+,

Paramount+, HULU, Tubi, Amazon Prime and iTunes, we are still forced to live in those moments as adults, explaining our petty to twenty-year-olds weekly! By us being the first, there were *plenty* of mistakes made. Some moments we would love to forget, but that made us all iconic OGs.

Keeping it real, *College Hill* revitalized on a national level the interest and excitement around historically Black colleges and universities in general. America had not really been seeing HBCUs depicted in any major television and programming besides *A Different World*. Now years later, we have shows like *All American: Homecoming*. Beyonce's Netflix special *Homecoming* was an entire show themed around HBCU culture at Coachella and it really brought the Black college experience into mainstream culture. It created interest and manifested other projects. The show also created additional opportunities for some of today's leading Black executives in entertainment! Behind the camera, production included reality TV producer, Carlos King, and now BET executives, Tiffany Lea and Connie Orlando who were producers on the show during its original airing. All of this wouldn't have existed without *College Hill*.

It's amazing to know that *College Hill* is now acknowledged as the first Black reality TV series! We are Black history. Thank you, BET and Tracey Edmonds!

About Ray Cunningham

If anyone keeps it real, it's Ray Cunningham, also known as Misster Ray. He is an award-winning bestselling author, social influencer, reality TV star, host and now actor best known for his ground-breaking and historic participation on America's first ever Black reality TV series, *College Hill*. As BET's first ever gay network talent, he appeared regularly on VH1's *Love & Hip Hop Hollywood* from 2017 to 2019.

Known as everyone's over the top friend in their head with no filter, he has established himself on various platforms, including TV (recurring contributor on TMZ & Roland Martin's award-winning *News One Now* talk show); movies (*You Married Dat? & The Assistant*); radio (WCDX Power 92 in Virginia & WKYS 93.9 in Maryland); and digital media (hosted and executive produced WEtv's award-winning longest running digital series Reality Wrap 2013-2018).

He is a proud two-time HBCU alum of Virginia State University located in Petersburg, Virginia, where he earned a bachelor's in mass communications and a master's in media management.

Throughout his 15+ year career in multi-media, Ray developed an extreme passion for HBCUs and political progress for minorities. To Ray, everything that deals with voting and getting the message out has a correlation to the media. Therefore, he is glad to be able to combine two of his passions for a common goal through his platforms.

Aside from Ray's community service and busy career demands, he just recently received his master's degree in media management and now manages the responsibility of being an ambassador for the National College Resources Foundation's (NCRF) Black College Expo, assisting with recruiting high school students to attend HBCUs all around the country. Additionally, Ray released America's first ever Black college novelty board game, Yardopoly, which celebrates HBCU culture and history.

As a celebrated notable public figure in his hometown, Ray was awarded Richmond Black Pride's Community Media Award and was presented a proclamation from the City of Petersburg by the mayor for his humanitarianism and community efforts. He was recently announced as one of the 2023 recipients of the Biden/Harris Presidential Award for Community Service, which he will be awarded along with an honorary doctorate's degree in Humanitarianism from Leaders Esteem Christian Bible University.

With Ray balancing his commitments both personally and professionally, he continues his work of systemically helping his community and strengthening his platform for better civic engagement while strengthening minority representation in various forms of media.

KINDA ANDREWS SAUNDERS
Most School Spirited

TV Pioneers

Kinda Andrews Saunders
Season 1

As a little girl from south Louisiana, I thought Miss Magnolia, Whitley Gilbert, was the most fabulous Southern Belle. Actually, I felt naturally connected to many of the characters at the fictitious Hillman College. You see, *A Different World* was not so different to me. The view of an HBCU was more like my reality. My name is Kinda Andrews Saunders, from Season One of BET's *College Hill*. Long before America's first all-Black reality show premiered in 2004, I practically grew up on the campus of Southern University and A&M College in Baton Rouge, Louisiana. Home of the Jaguars.

My story begins two generations before my conception, when my grandfather Thomas J. Smith attended Southern University on the G.I. Bill after World War II. My grandpa was the first person in our family to go to college. This was a time when a historically Black college and university was not a boldly deliberate option. It was the only option. My mother, Agnes Smith, followed in her father's footsteps, graduating from Southern. Later, she met my father Donald Andrews who was also a Southern graduate. After my parents married, and my father acquired his Ph.D., they decided to start a family. Enter, Me! Even as a middle child, I like to think I was the baby jaguar my family always wanted.

My childhood is virtually spilling over with memories from SU. Traveling to the football games, eating nachos and hot sausages in the stadiums, those red sausages that make your mouth burn, are some of the best memories. Shaking my blue and gold pom poms as fast as my hands could manage, imitating the dancing dolls during halftime, singing along as the Human Jukebox played the alma mater. After all, they are the best band in the land. Our family of five rarely missed a Bayou Classic. I guess it's a no brainer that I chose to attend the only university for me. In the fall of 2003, I became a third-generation jaguar.

Only a few days after moving into my dorm, Washington Hall, my dorm-mates said they were holding auditions for a new TV show in the Smith-Brown Memorial Union. I was just tagging along to enjoy the camaraderie. Eventually, I decided to go in for an audition since I was already waiting in line. I remember being authentic and having fun during the audition. I've never really been one to bite my tongue. It was this extroverted approach that caught the casting team's interest. That and the fact that my father was, and still is, the longest serving Dean of Southern's College of Business, while I was clearly a rebel without a cause. Within minutes of leaving the audition, I got a phone call. They offered me a spot on the cast.

I remember the very first day we began filming. I didn't have any experience or any prep time. The director called and told me to meet the camera crew in my dorm lobby. I was by myself, and I was so nervous! I was an eighteen-year-old freshman who had just moved to campus. There were camera people and a lobby full of students waiting for me to walk into the room. Sheesh! Talk about butterflies. Luckily, I have a background in theatre. So, even when I'm most nervous, I can usually "act" brave.

We did not waste much time getting into a groove with making the show. Our co-ed cast of four guys and four girls quickly moved into an on-campus suite where we lived, worked and bonded together in Shade Hall. It was not until the show premiered on January 28, 2004, that things really hit us. We weren't just running amok, playing on campus anymore. Our hijinks were being broadcast into households across the nation. People recognized us in the store. People had opinions about us, especially people who didn't really know us, but they thought they knew us. There was definitely a steep learning curve to deal with that reality. Personally, I learned to grow thick skin, to hold my head high, and to know my worth was not wrapped up in anyone else's opinion of me. I also learned that the people who love you will love you regardless. Like my husband, Charles Saunders, the first guy I met on campus and my love interest featured on *College Hill*. This is a life lesson I will always carry with me. Now, Charles and I carry these lessons on in raising our six children.

Undoubtedly, each cast member learned something. They learned some lessons in their own way. That's one way we are all alike. We had our differences, our own roles to play, but there is still a connected feeling. It's almost like we were part of a 'social experiment' together. Because of that, we share a link that is timeless. Even now, whenever I talk to my former cast members, it's as if no time has passed. We still feel like a little family almost twenty years later. That speaks to the magnitude of what we accomplished. It's surreal that I thought we were just college kids going to school. Lo and behold, it was actually something much more. I don't know if we realized it at the time, but what we did was historic. We were true reality TV pioneers. There was no script or crafted storylines. We were really just living our lives. We lived our truths.

Never before had there been an all-Black reality TV show. Our different world was our real world. The wild child, the jock, the nerd, the rich girl, the class clown, the beauty queen, the country girl and the frat boy. It was amazing to see how we all learned to live together. If the authorities ever let Season One of *College Hill* out of the vault, you will see exactly what I am talking about. If not, well, you just had to be there.

About Kinda Andrews Saunders

Hailing from Baton Rouge, Louisiana, Kinda Andrews Saunders is the middle of her parents' three children. In classical middle child fashion, Kinda has always been an extrovert, drawn to the light. Kinda asserts her amazing mentors were her very own parents. Her father is Dr. Donald Andrews, the longest serving Dean of Southern University's College of Business. Her mother, Agnes Andrews, is a thriving entrepreneur with one of the top performing Allstate agencies in the state of Louisiana. Growing up at events on Southern's campus and attending Southern University Laboratory School gave Kinda a front row seat into what the HBCU life could be, and she loved it. Kinda attended Southern University, where she was a cast member of BETs *College Hill*, the first ever Black reality TV show, making television history. Kinda married her college sweetheart, Charles Saunders, and they traveled the continental U.S. during his time as a naval seaman. They now have six children. Kinda and her family have appeared in national commercials and ads, and they have even gone viral on more than one occasion. This led Kinda to the realm of social media influencing and eventually social media marketing. Her efforts garnered enough attention to land a pilot for her own television docuseries. Now, Kinda has established ThatKindaLuv, LLC.

Kinda says, "It wasn't until becoming a mother that I realized legacy is the most important thing we have and the most important thing that we leave behind. Our legacy is the mark we can leave on the world and my children are my legacy. I believe we must sow into our young ones so that we become better with each generation."

GABRIEL D. LANGLEY "JY"
Most Likely to Be Phrozen

The Start of Something Great
Gabriel D. Langley "JY"
Season 1

My college experience was what I hoped it would be, but it was also quite different from what I thought it would be. Attending Southern University, my first introduction was crab week in the band. And although I heard the stories and the rumors, it was still more mentally demanding than I could have imagined. The expectations from my fellow band members and freshman crab brothers were unwavering. No one gave you a pass. No one accepted your excuses either. You were either good enough, or you weren't. Although my personality was always to be the best, it was a jaw-dropping reality that now I was in a room full of talented individuals, and my best was no longer good enough. The challenge was on.

The first semester of my academic year is mostly a blur because of how much time I spent adjusting to band life of this caliber. However, the friends and relationships that we built in that band room were forged forever. Dr. Isaac Gregg was a pure inspiration because he always expected everything from you. His motto that molded my personality for the next four years and beyond was, "Be at the right place at the right time with the right equipment, ready to concentrate." I attended Southern University on a music scholarship, and my degree course was Biology and Music Performance. I found mentors and inspiration in many different professors over the years. Musically, the other associate band director, Mr. Lawrence Jackson, taught me that your energy is contagious. If you're having fun, so will those you are there to entertain. Associate Director Mr. Cornell Knighten told us, "Demand your worth, but never sacrifice your integrity." Mr. Alvin Baptiste taught me the passion behind New Orleans jazz and improvisation. Academically, I was pushed to be better by Dr. Willis Jacob and Dr. Fitzgerald Spencer of the Biology

Department, which helped me achieve multiple Honor Society inductions and to receive an invitation to the 2005 Endocrinology Symposium in San Diego, California. This also led to me being one of the representatives for Southern University at the BKX and NIS Conference in Richmond, Virginia in 2005 and being invited to the Endocrinology Symposium in San Diego, California in 2005. Lastly, my worldview and social ideology were turned upside down when I took a mandatory cultural class: the African American Experience (Psychology) with Dr. Reginald Rackley.

Everything you thought you knew about your Blackness was challenged as his curriculum exposed you to the unknown influences of today's society. For me, it has been one of the more significant factors contributing to navigating my life, utilizing my social circles, and gauging my success. Having professors see your potential, and their willingness to be a resource to you, meant everything to me. They gave me structure and forced me to elevate my character to the person they saw in me. Yes, I partied with the best of them. Yes, I lived the Greek life and won step shows with Alpha Phi Alpha and Kappa Kappa Psi Band Fraternity. However, when I reflect on my college experience, I realize how demanding my professors were of my success and how invested they were in me to rise to the challenge. This, to me, was the HBCU Experience.

In the early fall of 2003, there was a buzz around campus about a pilot reality TV show being filmed. Little was known or seen, but everyone knew it was happening. Then, as the official school year kicked off, it became evident that BET had a reality TV show planned for students on campus. They were holding auditions to fill the cast. I had no interest in being a part of any reality show. But one day, the casting crew showed up in the band room. Later, I learned that they were looking for a cast member to highlight Greek life on campus. And, in grand fashion, Dr. Greggs said, "KK Psi and band is the biggest fraternity on campus. If you want to capture the Greek experience, then you need to follow the Southern University Band."

Of course, we all cheered in agreement until we realized we all had to undergo the long interview process. Again, not having much desire to be on the show, I went through the motions and answered their questions. Then, the band went outside to perform a show for them to get visuals on everyone they were interested in. After that, the idea was no more than an afterthought. About a week later, I received a phone call asking if I was interested in the show. By this time, my tuition situation had changed. I lost part of my scholarship due to a clerical error and could not pay for housing. I was currently sleeping on the hard floor of my frat brother's dorm room. They wanted me to join the cast since I was in the band, plus KK Psi, Alpha Phi Alpha, and somewhat entertaining. I just needed that room and board to get off that cold floor. So, I packed my things and moved into the dorm room set on campus.

Our season was heavily based on following eight students as they experienced everyday college life at an HBCU. The camera crews followed us to class. They followed us to events on campus and off campus, and they filmed us interacting with each other as cast members (good, bad, and ugly). We created many memories and moments. But there are a few that stand out the most to me. The first one was our fan boat tour of the Louisiana bayou. This was an experience like no other, jumping on a fan boat and cruising through the narrow creeks of the Louisiana swamp land and witnessing all of the crazy interesting lifestyles that go along with it. It was a family-owned and operated business that took us on the Bayou Tour. To this day, we all talk about the patriarch of the family, whom they enduringly called Cappy (Captain-Pappy). He was an older man with a spry step. He spoke with a heavy accent in what seemed to be a mix between Southern twain and French that seemingly only his son could understand. Everyone laughed when he laughed—not because we knew what he said funny—but because we couldn't understand him, and he laughed so hard, showing off his one or two teeth in front. No greater memory of that day stands out than when Cappy was showing us how to feed the flathead catfish of the bayou with dog food. Delano leaned over the edge of the boat to get a better look at the fish, and his cell phone stored in his top shirt pocket took a swim in the dark and muddy water. Yes, it was gone for good, and yes, Cappy laughed, so we laughed, except for Delano.

Another great memory was when we, as a cast, got in trouble for not obeying the rules for keeping the production team up to date on our whereabouts and agendas. It wasn't intentional. But for most of us, we were juniors and seniors. So, we were always on the go. Having to tell someone where we were going, what we were doing, and who we were going to be with seems like a return to parental supervision. So, the production team decided to get their point across by having the drill sergeant for the Marine ROTC give us his version of punishment with 5 a.m. PT and team building. As you would expect, he and his team came in, yelling and waking everyone up. They were no joke. It quickly became physical with the push-ups, sit-ups, running, and carrying the team tree log. Everyone still had crust in their eyes, and the ladies had their hair tied up from sleep. However, I was fresh off a night of partying and had just walked through the door at 4 a.m. So, it was all jokes to me. They didn't like me laughing at the camera.

We had fun on top of fun and made memories that we laugh about to this day. But during that time, we had no idea of the impact and history we were making for HBCU campuses nationwide. We didn't realize we were the first all-Black cast reality TV show until commercials started rolling out. I literally had news reporters sitting in my living room during the first episode watch party. That premiere season of *College Hill* on BET quickly became the number one show on the network. After hundreds of interviews and news articles about this "all-Black cast" reality show, we noticed the positive impact of youth interest in HBCUs.

Edmond entertainment and BET found a creative way to dismiss the stigmas of attending a historically Black college and university by highlighting the everyday life of eight college students being positive, attending classes, parties, events, being sociable, and being involved on campus. They showed students enjoying Greek life, cheer life, athletic life, and being popular—or not so popular. Most importantly, they show that it is okay to be all those things or none of those things as you journey through college to find yourself. The enrollment at SU increased beyond expectations that fall semester, and the internet's outcry for another season was proof that we had started something great.

About Gabriel D. Langley "JY"

Gabriel D. Langley is a creative and spirited personality from Dallas, Texas who uses his gift in the business and entertainment worlds. He attended Southern University and A& M College in Baton Rouge, Louisiana, where he initially studied Biology and Music Performance. With entertainment being a big part of his life, in 2004, he began pursuing a career in entertainment professionally.

Gabriel got his start as a model with notable work, posing for *Dobbs & Krave Magazine*, runway shows for Coogi, photoshoots for Ed Hardie, and collaborating with great stylists such as Rick Davy (NY) and Tracy Kennedy (LA). Under the alias, Gabriel D. Angell, he's performed on trumpet with Tito "TJ" Jackson, Jr., Rickey Smiley, Erykah Badu, Tichina Arnold, and Groove University Live Band. Gabriel has performed on drums with Mark Hildreth, J-Pop Artist Takao, NY77 L.A. Funk Band, and others. As an actor, Gabriel has starred and featured in several films, including *Spades-4 Of A Kind, Black Angels, Searching the Movie, He Heard My Cry, Mouthpiece, Sex & Violence*, and *Walter*. He also has made television appearances on shows such as *Blood Relatives, Friday Night Lights*, the Original Season of BET's *College Hill* at Southern University, and the hit German Detective TV Series *Carsten Stahl-PrivatDetektiv*.

Gabriel is also a serial entrepreneur, starting with his sports fitness and in-home personal training service in 2005 and musician management in 2006. As a foundation for his entrepreneurial spirit, he worked to develop trade-in credit development and finance. This trade opened the door to contract and consulting work. Gabriel quickly diversified his non-traditional financial education by collaborating with companies such as Debt Relief America and Westlake Financial Services, and consulting with New Sky Funding and Out of Box Business Funding & Development. Gabriel then advanced to his current role as partner at AG Management & Business Consulting, working with small businesses on strategic management and business relationships.

After years of investing and working with startups, Gabriel looked for a franchise opportunity and fell in love with being an authorized dealer for FUBU Mobile. Yes! The clothing brand. A couple of years later, Gabriel and his business team were granted control of the Master Agency and Business Operations. Now that FUBU is "in the business of connecting people," he and his teams' current goal is to elevate FUBU Mobile by growing the brand's trust in the telecommunication industry, promoting economic growth and championing social unity in the community. For Us, By Us/For Unity, By Unity. As Gabriel continues to manage and consult with businesses, he decided to return to school and pursue a post-graduate education in Business Psychology.

Gabriel ultimately wants to be an asset to the communities that have helped groom him over the years. He wants to continue to grow his involvement in uplifting those in need with his nonprofit company, Village Inspiration Project (V. I. P.). Gabriel looks forward to building on the work he's done and using his connections and resources to break down barriers holding aspiring youth from achieving success.

VERONICA MOSS
Most Likely To Be a Devastating Diva

The Amazing HBCU Experience
Veronica Moss
Season 1

Being the middle child of six kids, I was always one to carve my own path and make bold choices. Some right, some wrong. But one I know was the right choice for sure was attending an HBCU. But not just any HBUC. The Southern University. A proud Houstonian, born and raised, there was always a special place in my heart for Louisiana, spending time each summer in Maurice, Louisiana, horseback riding with my cousins, learning the pride in land ownership and farming—values still instilled in me to this day. In fact, my parents still laugh and joke about my "organic, why?," "pesca'-what?-tarian" lifestyle. They want to know what's wrong with the "bacon" I was raised on. Little do they know, my passion for understanding healthy food, cooking and traveling to remote getaways started with my roots in Louisiana.

Growing up, I attended predominantly white schools. My parents, being first-generation entrepreneurs, raised us in Sugar Land, a suburb of Houston. It's worth mentioning the fact that we don't credit our Black baby boomers who were figuring out how to raise kids in the burbs with a whole different level of diversity and no true community in the neighborhood. They knew, if nothing else, they had to get us involved in church, Jack & Jill, and Top Teens. You name it, we did it. In order to ensure we knew who we were, and that we didn't get lost in the 80s/90s suburb boom filled with sounds of Nirvana, M3s on the student parking lot, penny loafers, and Ralph Lauren backpacks.

I always valued individuality. Never one to have one set of friends or a clique, per se. Once again, I was carving my own path. I knew by my sophomore year in high school that I wanted two things: to go out of state and to attend an HBCU. My first options were Howard and Clark, but my folks were nervous about having me move that far away. Then, one of my school counselors introduced me to Southern University. I knew I couldn't go along with the status quo of limiting myself to the belief that predominantly white institutions (PWIs) were the only route to success. I knew Southern was out of state, and it was one of the top 20 HBCUs in the country in 2001. I knew I'd have the opportunity to make lifelong friendships.

So, there I was, August of 2002. I was officially a freshman. Not just a college freshman, but I was a freshman in life. I was in a new city, away from home, and completely responsible for who I would become. I carved out the first steps in developing a career path. Culture shock ensued on arrival, outside of a concert, car show (yeah, y'all remember those), or party. I had never been around thousands of my Black peers, all on the same path, yet on different journeys. It was my time. How did I close out the first semester? With a fight with a roommate, of course! By December, I was done with Southern in my mind. My dad introduced me to my first strategic decision-making lesson. He said, "I'll tell you what. You can come home, and your dorm will be upstairs in your room. You'll have a curfew after class, and that's that." So where was I in January? Back at Southern! His guidance was right. By the end of the second semester, I had made new friends. I was on the Dean's List, confirmed my major being Marketing, and was all set on my path to eventually graduate.

At the start of my sophomore year, word was out. There was a new show coming to BET called *College* Hill, and Tracey Edmonds was coming to campus to host auditions. I thought it sounded cool, but I didn't think it would be something I would be interested in doing, nor did I have the time to do it. I was walking from class one afternoon, and one of the producers of the show walked up to me and said, "You've got to come and meet the team. We'd love to interview you for the show." Initially, I said, "No way!" But then, I listened to the fact that *College Hill* was all about showing the HBCU experience from different perspectives and encouraging other promising students to attend. I thought about it and interviewed that afternoon. An hour later, I received a callback that I was cast.

Within a week, I went from being a too shy to even participate in the show nineteen-year-old to moving into the "real life, a couple of strangers with a confession booth" house, with 24/7 cameras twenty years prior to the TikTok and Instagram boom—where documentaries and reality TV were essentially the closest thing to real people and real, everyday experiences being shown on TV. I was so nervous. But I soon met some of the most interesting people. When you are in a living situation with strangers, you don't have the opportunity to stay in the mindset of, "It's all about me." You realize that everyone has their own experience in life. I learned about meditation and healing practices that I initially judged. I shed tears hearing the story of a strong young mom-to-be. All of us talked about generational trauma before it was even considered. As roommates, we shared stories about the weight we felt and the fervent desire to overachieve in all things—not only as young Black women and men—but as Black children. Most of us were the first, second or third generation in our families that even had an opportunity or choice to attend college, be athletes, and leave home.

It was transformative, and I felt like I grew so much in that semester. It was so much more than a bunch of students being on camera. This was bigger than us. We were representing the first generation of HBCU students on TV, opening the door and providing a view to show that we worked hard, while still having fun, but overall pursuing wonderful things. When I look back at my time on *College Hill*, and my time overall at Southern, I wouldn't have changed a thing. From the professors who taught me more life lessons than rhetoric, to the faculty and staff that treated me like family, there was no shortage of mentors when on "the yard." To the importance of creating excellence within myself, and being my own boss, I graduated humble, yet confident, in knowing that if I could make it at Southern, I could make it anywhere. I stand on it to this day.

Even twenty years after the initial show aired, there isn't a year that goes by where so many people tell me how Season 1 encouraged them to go to Southern or an HBCU, or how it was a catalyst for building the intrigue to bring HBCUs to mainstream conversations. Looking back, my HBCU experience was amazing—from the lifelong friendships, my line sisters (now forever sisters) of Delta Sigma Theta, hosting Rip the Runway at the iconic Spring Bling, to the leaders I came across who inspired me. I wouldn't trade it for anything. Despite life's challenges, and overcoming them professionally and personally, I can always credit my experience to "the experience—*College Hill* x Southern University."

About Veronica Moss

Veronica Moss is a native of Houston, Texas, and the proud mother of Harper. As a graduate of Southern University and A&M, she is a dedicated professional who has built a career on taking risks and stepping out on faith. Shortly after earning a Bachelor of Science in Marketing, she left her hometown for Atlanta, without employment, but armed with knowledge, passion and ambition. Within weeks, Veronica was hired by Moroch, one of the top advertising agencies in the world.

Currently, Veronica is a Senior Product Manager for Cox Communications. Before her tenure with Cox, Veronica built a very impressive career in Marketing Strategy and Business Consulting across the U.S. Veronica's extensive and diversified background includes sixteen years of defining and delivering successful enterprise software products, leading cross-functional teams, and in-depth knowledge of product life-cycle management. Ever progressing product innovation, her strengths lie in her ability to maximize outreach potential and lead go-to-market executions.

She has previously implemented marketing campaigns for several national companies, such as NRG Energy, Centurylink, Waste Management and McDonald's. Her work also includes government and municipal agencies such as Louisiana Economic Development and Houston Metro. Lastly, Veronica devotes her time to several of her daughters' school organizations, and she is a member of Delta Sigma Theta Sorority, Inc.

DELANO HOLMES
Most Likely to Set It Owt

"O Southern, Dear Southern"
Delano Holmes
Season 1

As far back as I can remember, I've always been intrigued by the Black College Experience. Having grown up in Los Angeles, California, shows like *A Different World* and movies like *School Daze* further sparked my interest in HBCUs. I was afforded the opportunity to attend The Southern University and A&M College in Baton Rouge, Louisiana in the fall of 2000. Being from LA, the HBCU scene was somewhat of a culture shock. There were beautiful shades of brown everywhere. The different accents, dialects, style of clothing and all-around swag was mind blowing. With most of my family being from south of Louisiana, I was aware of both Southern University and Grambling State University. However, being aware and actually walking the yard were two different situations. It was always a dream of mine to be on television, so I decided initially to major in theater. After a little research, I chose journalism as my focus of study. With football being my secondary focus, I dreamed of playing in The Bayou Classic, which I had watched on television since I was a little kid. I have four older cousins who went to Grambling University, and they all played football. They always bragged about The Bayou Classic experience. This was something I really looked forward to.

My first semester at Southern was cool. I finished the semester on The Dean's List and looked forward to the spring semester. Unbeknownst to me, that fall semester was filled with occurrences, one in which I had no way to prepare for, nor could I even imagine it happening. My mother, Constance Marie Holmes, passed away. I was a freshman in college. Suddenly, I was faced with the task of raising a nine-year-old little brother. The world as I knew it had drastically changed. For the first time in my life, I doubted myself. I figured that

I would not be able to continue college and achieve the goals that I set forth prior to attending Southern University. I questioned myself, "Can I do it? How will I make it by myself? Can I afford this? Will I ever be on TV? Will I be successful? How do I enjoy this experience and be a positive role model to my little brother?"

There are a lot of things in this world for which I am grateful. One of them is Pearlie Mae Brown. My grandmother and ace boon coon. Pearlie Mae stepped right on up and told me that she had my back 100%. I had a goal to accomplish, and she would do her best to make sure I kept my promise to my mother. So, we kept striving.

By this time, I was in the full swing of things. Honestly, I dropped the ball with the whole football thing. No pun intended. But man was I grooving! Baton had a lot to offer at the time and I had my hand in all of it. I started seriously rapping and took a shot at acting. I was always the funny class clown-type, so it came naturally. I formed a group called The Imitators. I was a master beat boxer and could sing fairly good. The group imitated different artists and songs while bringing a comedic element to each performance. My brother Y. Luck (Keith Swanier) and Justin "DJ JUICE" Patterson formed the group. We entered five talent shows. We won all five and never looked back. By now, my name was buzzing around campus. Like on *School Daze*, the brothers of Omega Psi Phi caught my eye. Around this same time, there was talk around the yard about a reality TV show audition.

Over the years, we heard talks of shows and movies coming to campus. So, initially, we thought it was just another fly by chance situation. But, to everyone's surprise, BET was on campus and in full effect. There were long lines in the student union as students filled out applications. These applications were at least twenty pages long. I grabbed one, filled out the first page, and wrote phrases I dare not repeat. Meanwhile, BET was also doing a little leg work, moving around campus and asking for the popular students on campus. My name came up numerous times.

I looked at myself as the heavyset Dwayne Wayne with way more swag. But seriously, I was initially selected to interview for the show. During the interview, I met Tracey Edmonds. I made up a story, telling Tracy that I was singlehandedly responsible for Babyface's success and that I was the person who gave him the name Babyface. Tracey replied as if she was astonished to never hear that story. Others in the room laughed as Tracey realized that I wasn't even born when he got started. I was instantly in. From there, we shot a pilot with me and seven other students. The pilot was a hit; however, they needed to replace a few of the cast members. Eventually, the cast was set, and it was time for filming. We all moved on campus into dorms. We filmed for the most part of the fall 2003 semester. At the same time, I was participating in membership selection with the brothers of Omega Psi Phi. Our initiation probate premiered on the last episode of the season.

The cast was full of characters. Surprisingly, we all got along really well as a cast. Relationships were developed that we still have today. I wasn't the oldest in the cast, but I had an old soul. So, many times I shared wisdom with my fellow castmates. I guess you can say I was Big Brother. I tried my best to uplift as much as possible.

Filming, social life and our scholastic responsibilities made it difficult at times; however, I wouldn't trade the experience for the world. *College Hill* premiered in the spring of 2003. It was an instant success. Millions of Black teens were afforded the opportunity to see firsthand what it was like to attend an HBCU. We were instantly famous. My little brother went to school every day and bragged about how his Big Brother was a TV star. And my Granny! Good Lord, my grandmother would brag and tell all her friends at church and in the community that her baby was on TV. She would say, "Girl, my grandbaby on the BET." I was extremely proud of the fact that we were actually able to go to my grandmother's house and film a couple of episodes. That meant a lot to me. For that, I am forever grateful.

Being on the first season of *College Hill* was a blessing. We were the first of its kind: an all-Black college reality TV series. I thank Tracey Edmonds and BET for the opportunity to launch my career. After *College Hill*, I went on to star in multiple films and sitcoms. I received my degree in the fall of 2005. I was able to keep my promise that I made to my mother four years prior. I was also able to stand as a true testament of what hard work and dedication can do. No matter what you're faced with, if you put your faith in God and stay determined, there's no limits to what you can accomplish. I continue to act, write and produce films and television shows in Los Angeles. I also currently have two businesses in the Los Angeles area, a cosmetic line called SASSY SUGA, and a New Orleans- style food eatery that specializes in New Orleans-style snowballs called SNEAUX BIDNESS. I am a brand ambassador and creative lead for DOPEAHOLIC, a nationwide cannabis company that focuses on bringing awareness to the culture, lifestyle and brand.

With the success of *College Hill*, many doors of opportunity opened, and I was able to inspire thousands of youths nationwide to attend HBCUs. Most importantly, I was able to inspire my little brother. As an adult, I chose human services as an addition to my entertainment work. I invest in people and help people overcome setbacks through a homeless service company called Volunteers of America. That love, understanding and care are all characteristics of that old, southern spirit, which I learned at my HBCU. I am blessed and overly grateful.

About Delano Holmes

Delano Mitchell Holmes is an actor, comedian, writer and entrepreneur from Los Angeles. He has enjoyed success in television and film for close to eighteen years. Once considered the "Black Belushi" by theatre Professor M. Rutland (Southern University School of Arts), Holmes has been able to deliver knee-slapping humor to audiences for years. Most recently, he can be seen aside Slink Johnson playing Detective Mitchell in the movie *Dirty Cops LA* (2021). He has also entertained audiences as "Avery" in the movie *A Gift Horse* and as "Spook" in *Da Block Party*.

Delano was raised in South Central, Los Angeles by his mother, Constance Marie Holmes. As a youth, he was faced with the daily trials of an African American man growing up in the inner cities of Los Angeles. As a product of a single-parent home, Delano was determined to succeed in both academics and athletics as a student at Westchester High School. It was his goal to not only excel in the classroom and on the football field, but to stand as a positive role model to his younger brother, Mark Lawson. Delano graduated high school with honors and chose "The" Southern University A&M College to further his collegiate academics. Delano received his B.A. in Journalism from Southern University and A&M College in 2005, as he had promised his mother he would after her sudden death in January of 2001.

While at Southern, Delano was an active member of The Southern University Student Government Association, Men's Federation and Southern University football team. In the fall of 2003, Delano was initiated into the Beta Sigma Chapter of Omega Psi Phi Fraternity, Inc. In that same year, Delano made his acting debut on BET's *College Hill*, which was the first all African American reality TV series. Later that year, he co-starred as "Spook" in the 2004 movie, *Da Block Party*. Since then, Delano has appeared in over sixteen films and two television series. During his eighteen-year acting career, he has worked with Chevy Chase, Mike Epps, Richard Dreyfus, Sherman Helmsley, Lou Diamond-Phillips, Clifton Powell, Carl Anthony Paine, Darrin Henson, Persia White, Joe Torry, Tracey Edmonds, Meagan Good, Ruby Dee, and John Snyder.

After graduation, Delano taught grade school English and Theatre in schools in New Orleans. As an entrepreneur, Delano focused on bringing the southern customs and traditions to Los Angeles. In 2020, Delano opened the first Sneaux Bidness, LLC, which is a New Orleans style eatery that specializes in New Orleans style Snowballs and cuisine. Delano is also co-owner of Sassy Suga Lips service, which is a beauty and health cosmetics brand located in L.A. Delano stands as a brand ambassador and creative lead of Dopeaholics, an L.A.-based lifestyle brand company that promotes culture and cannabis that believes in Making America Dope Again.

Delano currently works as a Program Manager for Volunteers of America in the greater Los Angeles area. He also oversees a National Youth Build program. That Youth Build program focusses on providing young adults aged 17-24 the opportunity to attain their high school diploma through John Muir Charter School. The program also offers construction and/or automotive trade through The Maxine Waters Employment Preparation Center located in Watts, California.

Delano has maintained a positive image in his community and professional career. He has homed in on his own craft and created a style of comedy that moves fluidly from scene to scene. Delano credits his grandmother, Ms. Pearl Mae Brown, for his hard work ethic, witty punchlines, and all-around crafty humor. Although he is able to portray a wide variety of dialects and personalities, many of the performances in his films are to pay homage to friends and family members of rural southern Louisiana. His family ties to the south allow him to capture those heartfelt, humorous, soulful characteristics of "down home" and bring those characters to life. As a man, his biggest task is to continue to stand as that positive role model for his brother and others in his family and community.

BRITTANI LEWIS
Most Likely To Be Voted #WCW

The Importance of Timing
Brittani Lewis
Season 2

My *College Hill* experience started out a bit crazy. It was a hectic day on campus, and I was already super emotional behind my big break up with Mr. Jacobs. I wasn't going to apply to be on the show. I was just going with my best friend who wanted to do the show. As soon as she started to apply, my ex showed up with his new girlfriend. Israel and I broke up and he started dating April. Israel was the hottest thing since sliced bread on the campus. So, everybody wanted him. I thought it would be best if I left, but my friend refused. She wanted me there. Throughout the chaos, the producer saw what was happening. One of the production assistants blurted out, "They used to date, but he dumped her to be with her."

That's what started the entire *College Hill* casting for me. I had to apply to be on the show. When I was cast, all these people from different areas of the United States came around. As we mingled, I noticed that we all got along, but we had many different points of views. It was extremely exciting, but I was a little confused. There had never been a black reality TV show before. It was so unexpected and new, but I was excited for it.

I got to meet people from all over the United States. For the most part, I had a good relationship with pretty much all of the cast, even though we had our differences. I loved it because this was something new for me.

Back then, no one really knew how to market. There was no social media. There was barely a Facebook. So, I think the experience overall for me was a bit surreal on one hand. I was excited to be able to do something so new and so different. But, on the other hand, I was wondering, "Where do I go from here?" I battled a bit after taping the show about what exactly I should be doing. I did the show. I had a bit of a fan base. But, because *College Hill* was so new, there was really no place for us in the industry due to the fact that reality TV really had no place yet.

I believe our season, Season 2, really put *College* Hill on the map. People were forced to pay attention. BET put us in a house compared to the Season 1 cast. They were taped on a campus. We got upgraded to MTV's *Real World* style. So, in doing that, we were taken seriously. The show taught a lot about friendships. It taught me that, at times, I don't know everything. It taught me that there's nothing wrong with listening and respecting someone else's opinion. There were many times we had tons of discussions about anything and everything. I learned to respect and understand other people's views. There's a bigger world out there.

We had a lot of fun times. We disagreed at some points and things got a little hectic. I was a bit crazy on the show. My ex-boyfriend got cast at the same time, so that was a bit interesting. But we're still friends today. People had never seen college students having the conversations and doing the things we were doing. We did feel the wrath of the backlash of our erratic behavior, but we were college students. After the show, there were times when I couldn't go to the store without being bombarded. I have never experienced anything like that before in my life. One time, I was with my family in Orlando. We went to the mall and a girl recognized me from the show. Immediately, so many people surrounded us. Eventually, we had to leave the mall. That's when I realized how big of an impact that we had made on a reality television show. We were just being ourselves. The scenes, the incidents, the conversations were all real. It was real television. It was not scripted. If I got to do it all over again, I wouldn't change a thing.

I'm glad I got the experience to do it. I got to actually see how I look, how I talk and how I behaved and reacted on television. Some of it I loved, but some of it shocked me. I got to see myself in a different light. During the taping, I was vulnerable. I was angry. There were times where I felt a bit of a loss trying to figure out if I was doing the right thing. The show left a positive impact on me simply because I have no regrets in my life, regardless of how hard it's been. I always look back and think about something so special happening to me that could've happened to any of the thousands of kids who wanted to apply to get on that show. They could've possibly been more interesting than me. But we see how things turn out.

The most positive impact *College Hill* had on my life has been timing. A lot of things did not make sense back then. The cast was young. The show was new. I learned that it might not always be a person's time, but I believe one must keep the faith, no matter how hard it gets. When your time does come, if you stay ready, you never have to get ready. Timing is everything to me. Overall, it was quite a ride. I'm grateful and thankful to have been a part of something so monumental. Fast forward to 2023. The world has completely changed. I'm excited to see what else I experience. After all, life is all about experiencing.

About Brittani Lewis

Brittani Lewis came to prominence after being casted on Season 2 of *College Hill* at Langston University, an HBCU out of Langston, Oklahoma in 2004. Majoring in Biology, she was excited to have such an opportunity her freshman year of college.

She is originally from Oklahoma City. Brittani currently is a successful real estate agent in Austin, Texas. She serves her community and is a member of the Austin Board of Realtors. Before her move to Austin, Brittani owned and operated an after-school program in north Dallas to assist working families with affordable childcare. Additionally, she owns a mobile health service and is a proud mother of two beautiful children.

While being on the show, little did she know that she would become a historic personality, making history as one of the first Black women on a black reality TV show. As she continues her success in business and her personal life with friends and family, she continues to make the impossible happen with upcoming projects and business yet to come.

RODNEY HENRY
Most Motivational

Unbreakable Bonds
Rodney Henry
Season 3

My college experience was nothing short of amazing. They were the best times of my life, besides having my kids. My college experience molded me to be more of a people person. I was more independent, and I simply learned how to navigate life and get things done, no matter what it is. I will figure out how to get it done. Virginia State University (VSU) diversified me. I feel like I can walk in any room and adjust to my environment. I found family at VSU, and friends that became siblings. We support each other like no other. Becoming a cast member of *College Hill,* "The First Black Reality Show," I didn't know the impact it would have on my life until the show aired. We really made history. We made college fun again. Viewers got to see it visually instead of hearing stories about someone's college experience.

It also put a spotlight on HBCUs, which, at times, we don't get the respect or the acknowledgment we deserve. Many of my favorite moments were giving back to the less fortunate and the parties. Experiencing this reality TV show with strangers allowed me to develop a bond with them. We did something none of us could have ever imagined: we made history being on a nationally televised Black reality show. Just the fact that the world got to know us gives me chills at times and makes me at a loss for words. I wouldn't take back one moment of it.

The funny thing about becoming a member of the cast of *College Hill* is that I wasn't going to do it because I didn't want people all in my business. So, I didn't come in for the interviews. But when other students were doing their interviews, they asked them who else would be a good fit for the show. Many of them recommended me to the producers.

Tracey Edmonds called me and said, "I'm not leaving this campus until I get an interview with you." So, I talked to my mother, brother and my friend LeGreg. I did the interview, and the rest is history. Being on the cast of *College Hill* presented me with several opportunities. I got to host *Rap City the Basement* and I hosted numerous events. I met Steven Hill in L. A., and I sat down with him at the table. He said, "I have some things in the works for you." Not really taking it too seriously until the following week, me and my older brother sat in his pink office in New York, and he told me to try out on *Rap City The Basement*. I felt like I was on top of the world. The one I was most excited about was when I got a call from *The Ellen DeGeneres Show*. I was hype. I ended up not getting that position, though. While hosting *Rap City*, I got to interview the legend, E-40. That was big for me.

BET used to look out and give us tickets to the BET Awards. Being interviewed on the red carpet was surreal. I had to pinch myself to make sure it was real. Seeing all the top artists perform, and some of them know who we are, man, you couldn't tell me nothing. After the awards, we had access to the after parties. I saw Snoop Dog walking across the street. I was dancing on the dance floor when I looked to my left and saw Suge Knight. We gave each other the "what's up" head nod and got back to dancing.

My life now is about family. It's all about taking care of my kids, making sure my wife is happy, and running my businesses while figuring out my next adventures. Being a father is something of which I am proud. If anybody knows me, they know my biological father didn't raise me. My Dad, who was my stepdad, raised me. I used to go through times where I didn't understand how my biological father had kids out here and didn't lose any sleep worrying about their welfare. It's inhumane if you ask me. So, when I had my kids, a day wasn't going to go by that I didn't know where they were, and they would always know where I was. I want to have a bond with my kids and instill something in their life. Some fathers don't have a bond with their kids, and I didn't want that. My oldest stays in Virginia Beach with his mom and is playing varsity football as a freshman. Now that I don't stay in Virginia, I still try to make it to half his games. When I can't make it, I watch his games via FaceTime from a family member who is in the stands. We talk every day. When we don't talk about sports, we talk about life or fishing.

My baby boy, who is almost two, lives with me and my wife in South Carolina. Being able to wake up to him every morning brings me joy. But taking care of my kids and being a father is something I take very seriously. Lastly, I still love a good vibe, whether that's fellowship with my family and friends, grabbing a drink at a sports bar, or just a night out on the town or a trip with friends. I will always find a way to enjoy life.

I want the readers to go to college and experience some of that Black college experience. You can gain so much in those four years and build some unbreakable bonds. Also, handle your business. Whatever your dreams and aspirations are, attack them. Learn your craft in and out. But have fun in the midst of doing it. Life is too short. Know the importance of fellowship. It's good for the soul!

About Rodney Henry

Rodney Henry grew up in Newport News, Virginia. After earning his degree in Sports Management, and wrapping up a stellar basketball career at Virginia State University in 2006, he set his sights on becoming a McDonald's owner/operator within FWL & Sons, Inc.

His hard work and experience led him to that achievement in 2012. Since then, he has expanded his entrepreneurial ventures as a silent investor in different businesses and start-ups, being co-founder of an event and entertainment company, and starting a real estate investment company.

Rodney and his wife, Fiori, now reside in Charleston, South Carolina, where he operates and owns McDonald's restaurants through the family business FWL & Sons, Inc. He is the proud father of two boys, Christian and Cairo. Rodney is a firm believer in community involvement and outreach programs, and he is a proud member of Phi Beta Sigma Fraternity, Inc. He has four brothers and a sister, enjoys outdoor activities, working out, and spending time with family.

BIANCA OLIVO
Most Likely To Spice Up Your Life

Grit, Perseverance and the Road Less Traveled
Bianca Olivo
Season 3

As a teenager, I dreamed of going to college and becoming a cheerleader. But growing up in a single parent household, with both financial and emotional struggles, that dream quickly faded. From the ages of about twelve to twenty-one, I was in and out of my home, staying with different friends and relatives, including my best friends Shana and Tiffany. Their mom, "Ma" as I called her, eventually convinced me to go to the vocational school to study cosmetology, but going to college was still the ultimate goal. Fortunately, after graduating high school, Shana and Tiffany went off to college at Virginia State University (VSU) and Elizabeth City State University, and I stayed behind. Working where I could and trying to make my way through life, I was only able to see the HBCU experience vicariously through them.

One day though, upon returning from college, Shana came home with great news. She had spoken to an admissions counselor at VSU about my situation and found a way for me to go to college without the assistance of my parents. Until then, I had never heard of a Historically Black College or University. All I knew was that I had the chance to go to college and make a better life for myself. So, I went through the application process, and that next fall, I was officially a VSU student.

The first week of school was a dream come true. I met diverse students from all around the world, joined clubs, and learned to "Never walk on the grass!" We even had a concert on campus featuring Chris Brown and Trey Songz. Deeper than that though was the opportunity to gain experience about the world from a more diverse perspective. My family took extraordinary pride in teaching me about my heritage: We are a combination of White from the Spaniards, Black from the Africans, and Taino from the Indigenous people of Cuba, Jamaica, Hispaniola (Haiti and the Dominican Republic), Puerto Rico and The Virgin Islands. But outside of my immediate family, I always felt like there was more to our history than the pilgrims and Indians, Christopher Columbus finding and conquering America, and the various wars taught in grade school. While my K-12 education prepared me to get into college, it also felt rather white-washed. Attending VSU broadened my knowledge of our history and gave me a unique perspective on the world around me. The HBCU experience was utterly amazing. Unfortunately, by the time I enrolled at VSU, I was already twenty-one and living well below the poverty level. I thought I would be able to support myself through school, but I couldn't even afford to live in the city that surrounded VSU. While I loved going to college, I simply couldn't afford it.

When the news broke about *College Hill* coming to our school, the campus was livelier than ever. I, however, had no idea what *College Hill* even was, and I was never really interested in being on TV; I had a car, so after finishing my homework at the library, I drove some of my friends from their auditions. One day while walking on campus, I got a call asking if I would be interested in coming to an audition. I wasn't sure how they got my number or how they even knew who I was. But my first instinct was to turn it down. After speaking with Shana and Tiffany, and them reminding me that I didn't have a housing option left for the rest of the semester, I changed my mind. I attended the last set of auditions, and the rest was history.

Literally. *History*. Who would have known that a show about college students just living life would be a hit, breaking records for BET?

The kids of *College Hill* became a family. We fought. We played games. We got into trouble. We pranked each other. We volunteered together and were there for each other. It was truly an experience like no other. I learned so much about life and myself that semester in school and on *College Hill* at the historic Ragland Mansion with the other roommates. I learned about social activism, giving back to the community and, most importantly, that we were all a work in progress. I know the show portrayed me as the sexy Puerto Rican party kitten. But the experience taught me that what others think of me does not define me. I learned that your body would show you signs of problems and disease if you took the time to pay attention to it. At that time, I did not know I was anemic. But I found out later that my embarrassing moments of sleeping past my time to work with the basketball team was actually due to severe anemia, along with other compounding medical conditions. I learned that life is a maze, and you never know who you will cross paths with. But we cross paths with people for specific reasons. It's funny because I never thought people liked me very much. Compared to the rest of the cast, I viewed myself as sort of an outcast. While I liked everyone, and I was friendly with everyone, Audrina became one of my best friends. We came from similar backgrounds where we had to work hard for everything we had. Life dealt us more punches than pushes forward. I was jealous of the rest of the cast as they came from more affluent backgrounds. However, our experience on the show was something only we could relate to.

My time on the show was extremely memorable. While we did take time to study and to party, we were also forced to integrate and really spend time with each other. This led to all kinds of food fights, the disastrous dinner date that never aired on TV, host a party where the proceeds went to charity, me holding a cute little Ninja Turtle hostage that I was unaware of the emotional value at the time, and have made amends with Will since then. It was an exciting time. We were young and free. We lived our lives unapologetically. Helping out at the food drive was the first time I had ever volunteered for charity. The house had a rotary phone (for the youthful crowd reading this, it is a telephone device from the past that had a large dial with numbers that you must rotate to dial the phone number).

While most people assumed *College Hill* was nothing but fun and games, the reason I cherish the experience so much is because we had a platform to show young Black and Brown kids that there is a college experience tailored specifically to them, which has boosted college enrollment in HBCUs. We were able to attend high schools in the Petersburg area and speak to youth from diverse backgrounds about going to college and our struggles, which has meant more young, Black and Brown kids are thinking about or planning to go to college. Over the years, fans have told me that our show was the reason they decided to go to college. The mere fact that my presence on *College Hill* allowed others to think about, or actually attend, college, is the biggest blessing from the show.

While I was not able to graduate from VSU, I went on to receive an Associate of Science in General Studies in 2009. In January of 2010, I set out to travel the world. I lived in Afghanistan and Dubai for almost three years, Colombia twice for two and a half years each. I even got an FAA Private Pilot's License before coming back to live in the U.S. I sought counseling several times over the years to continue to work on myself inside and out. In 2016, I started school again at the University of Phoenix and moved to the south. There I worked in the oil and gas industry while I completed my Bachelor of Science in Business with a Undergraduate Certificate in Project Management, which led me to Houston, Texas where I was reunited with Deirdra in 2018 who introduced me to a church that I would later attend, get baptized and volunteer at for about a year.

In the spring of 2022, I finally obtained a Master of Business Administration with a Graduate Certificate in Analytics. Later that summer of 2022, *College Hill: The Celebrity Edition* came to TSU, and I was able eat a nice lunch with Ray and Deirdra. Well, that lunch at Graces in Houston (I highly recommend it) turned into an all-night event as we barhopped while we caught up on the past few years. It was truly a blessing to be able to break bread with my fellow cast mates and to see how the events of their lives have played out since the time in the Ragland Mansion. Sitting with them recapping the moments of our last 15 years, I learned that my perception of myself was quite different than others' perception of me and that realization has inspired me to continue my mental health care routines to fortify self-love and appreciation. Currently, I am working for the Naval Facilities Engineering Systems Command's Atlantic Division as a Program Analyst.

If I had to identify one special thing from attending an HBCU and, specifically, VSU, it would be that people from Virginia have talent and people of color are tenacious and creative. Additionally, I learned that no matter what obstacles I'm faced with, there's always a creative way around them. I learned to open my mind to a world of possibilities I never dreamed were attainable. I learned to leverage my background and well-rounded education to out-whit those who might have the upper hand. Most importantly, I learned to be my true authentic self because beauty lies in authenticity. To this day, I take the experiences and lessons I learned while attending VSU and being on *College Hill: Season Three* to help guide and spread light to others.

Ephesians 5:8 (ESV) says, *"For at one time you were darkness, but now you are light in the Lord. Walk as children of the light."*

About Bianca Olivo

Bianca Raschell Olivo is a Mestiza Latina (a mixture of White, African and Taino). She was born in Virginia in 1984 and raised between Virginia Beach, Virginia, Caparra Tierra and San Sebastian, Puerto Rico. She attended Virginia State University in 2006 where she appeared as a cast member of *College Hill: Season 3* before ultimately getting an Associate of Arts degree in General Studies from Tidewater Community College in 2009. After obtaining her degree, she left the U.S. to travel the world, working with her father's aviation logistics company in Afghanistan, Dubai and Colombia in the areas of Human Resources, Health and Safety and Logistics. She gained a Federal Aviation Administration, Private Pilot License in October of 2012 while living and working overseas.

In 2016, she returned to the United States to finish school while changing careers from aviation to oil and gas. While working and attending school full-time, she graduated from the University of Phoenix in 2018, where she obtained a Bachelor of Science in Business and an undergraduate certificate in Project Management. In 2020, she returned to college at Louisiana State University, obtaining her Master of Business Administration with accompanying Graduate Certificate in Data Analytics, graduating with a 4.075 GPA. Currently, Bianca resides in Virginia Beach and is working as a Program Analyst for the Naval Facilities Engineering Systems Command.

KRYSTAL LEE
Most Popular

Culture Shock
Krystal Lee
Season 4

Initially, I joined *College Hill Season 4* because I wanted to be famous. I thought it would be an awesome opportunity to build my portfolio. I had always been a fan of reality television. Prior to *College Hill*, I appeared on *The Tyra Banks Show*, a Robin Thicke music video, and I even did some bikini modeling for Von Dutch. At the time that I was cast on *College Hill*, I was working full-time and going to community college full-time. So, naturally, I jumped at the opportunity to get an all-expenses paid semester away and gain more exposure. When it was confirmed that I would be part of the cast of *College Hill 4,* and living in the Virgin Islands, I was ecstatic! At this point, I had never been outside of the West Coast, let alone outside of North America.

I was a Black and Japanese girl being raised in Orange County, California, affectionately known as "The O.C." I grew up in predominately white neighborhoods. I was one of six Black children at my high school (two of them being my brother and cousin). Getting accepted to attend a historically Black college in The Virgin Islands was going to be a culture shock. Since I was attending a community college, studying for college away from home was quite an experience.

Being part of the *College Hill Season 4* cast changed my life. I attended a college where not only the students, but even the professors, looked like me. I was so happy to be surrounded by other like-minded Black students. I was able to learn so much from my time on the show and from my castmates. Each of my castmates were from unique backgrounds, and this opportunity allowed us to share our unique experiences. Being a Black American, or African

American, I was very naïve to the idea that Black people can come in many diverse cultures. I was only used to seeing the stereotypical southern Black culture that my family represented. *College Hill Season 4* introduced me to the rich culture of Afro Virgin Islanders. At times, I felt ill-equipped to manage a lot of the conversations and topics that we had on the show. Ultimately, I gained so much personal growth due to my time on the show. I honestly believe that, oftentimes, we are placed in uncomfortable situations to push ourselves to be better. My experience on *College Hill* was that uncomfortable push. It challenged me, and it made me better. The show taught me to be open and more accepting of distinct cultures and backgrounds. Bet's *College Hill* had, and still has, an enormous impact on Black youth. Over the years, I have had so many people reach out to me and say that the show was the reason they went to college or attended an HBCU.

Being a part of America's first Black reality TV show was the most amazing and memorable experience in my life. After the show aired, I was bombarded with fans. This was a time before the social media beast that we have today. Only Myspace and Facebook existed. I remember a time when I went to Virginia and visited my cousins, who were attending Hampton University. Everywhere I went, I was recognized and followed. Once we went to the local movie theaters, and we couldn't even watch the movie due to constant interruptions from fans of the show. At times, my popularity became overwhelming. I went from a regular college kid to a Black celebrity overnight.

Being on America's first Black reality TV show also had its benefits. I was living in L.A. after the show, so I was able to get so many exclusive invites to upscale functions and parties. My most memorable moment of being on the show actually happened *after* the show. We were at the 2006 Bet Awards as guests. My fellow castmate, Fallon, and I were escorted to the restrooms behind the scenes. We ran into Queen Bey herself: Beyonce. She called us by our names and told us that she loved watching our show. When I tell you that was the icing on top of the cake. You can't even imagine what it feels like to have your idol say that they love watching your reality TV show. That moment will forever live rent free in my mind. I was blown away that a huge mega celebrity even knew who I was!

There were even times I tried to lie and say I wasn't "Krystal from *College Hill*." I felt out of control of people's perception of me. After gaining my "celebrity" status, I realized that I did not want to pursue being in the limelight any further. I just wanted to be "regular" again. Fame does funny things to people; it will change you. No longer did I feel the urge to be known. At this point, I was infamous. Sometime after the show, I retreated from the television and went on to focus on myself.

Eventually, I attended California Baptist University in Riverside, California. I obtained both a bachelor's degree in business administration and a master's degree in business administration management. Before *College Hill*, I did not see myself obtaining any type of degree, let alone becoming a college graduate. I became the first woman to graduate college, and I was the first to get an MBA in my family. My participation on *College Hill Season 4* gave me the confidence I needed to further my educational goals.

I want other Black kids to know that college is obtainable. You don't have to come from money or have parents to support you. If you want something, get it for yourself! Dreams will become reality when you reach for them.

Today, I live in sunny Orlando, Florida with my son and my spouse. I work in Human Resources because I love to lend a helping hand and help others problem solve. To this day, I still get recognized by fans. I feel so humbled to have been a part of such history.

About Krystal Lee

Krystal Lee attended the University of the Virgin Islands (UVI) while filming BET's *College Hill Season 4*. After attending UVI, Krystal decided to follow her faith and enroll at California Baptist University in Riverside, California. She went on to complete back-to-back programs in business, where she achieved a bachelor's in business administration and a master's in business administration. Today, Krystal focuses on helping others and making a difference through her career as a Human Resources generalist in the fitness world.

WILLIE MACC
Class Clown

Life of MacC
Willie Macc
Season 4

In high school, I didn't even think about college. I graduated from high school with a 1.9 GPA. I didn't care about college. Just like in church, I went to sleep in class because the words danced around, and my teachers couldn't excite me enough to learn. I finished high school, and I didn't know what to do. I didn't want to work at that clothing store for the rest of my life!

I was a preacher's kid and extremely sheltered. My mom and dad never watched slave movies. I didn't see *The Color Purple* until I was in my thirties! My parents never talked about the importance of Black culture and being black. At that time, I thought being black sucked. Because I was dark-skinned, people made fun of me more. People told me I wasn't attractive as the light-skinned guy. So, I developed an inner hate for myself. The most I knew about Black culture was what I saw on BET late nights with the volume low. With a more conservative father, whatever we did watch on TV didn't really have "any seasoning" or flavor. Music-wise we listened to all Gospel. The first rap song I listened to was in seventh grade and it was Three 6 Mafia's *Chickenhead*. I became very curious. In high school, I got my then girlfriend pregnant. I thought this was my life. College wasn't in my future. I was just a silly kid who didn't know how to stay still. I wouldn't stop cracking jokes and I always got in trouble for it.

My dad told me to choose the Army or community college. We were at war in the middle east at the time. If my gun shooting skills were anything like my basketball shooting skills, I didn't need to be there. So, I decided to go to a community college to learn computer programming. That was the field my dad was in, and he made good money. I did basic coding. Then, the girl I was dating decided to take her modeling talent to Los Angeles. I was only eighteen. At the time, I was so in love. At nineteen, we decided to move. But we didn't have any money to live. We found a school that also had student housing. So, we went. Once there, I was finally free.

College life was cool. I missed so much living in L.A.! But I needed money to live. So, I did background work and that's where I met Bernie Mac in 2005. Because of him, I made my stage name Willie Macc instead of going by Willie McMiller. I got most of my gigs off Craigslist. One day, my friend Michael called me to tell me about *College Hill*. He thought I'd be a great fit. He told me if I could just be Willie, and make his sister laugh, I would pretty much be on the show.

I didn't understand the importance of an HBCU until I transferred over to UVI so I could be on the show. My girlfriend didn't want me to be on *College Hill* because she thought I'd have too many groupies. A week before I left, I got a call from Sean Rankine (showrunner EP) angry! He said, "Willie, this is so messed up! Why are you canceling on us? I know you said don't contact you anymore and this is your final decision. But I need to hear it from you. What happened?!" I was like, "I have no idea what you are talking about!" He said, "The email you sent, quitting the show!" I said, "Sean, I don't know what email you are talking about. Send it to me because I'm doing this show!" When he sent it to me, it read, "To Whom It May Concern: This is Willie McMiller. I was supposed to leave soon to go to the Virgin Islands, but I have changed my mind. After doing some soul searching, I will no longer be on this show. I apologize for the inconvenience. Thank you for understanding. Do not call me or email me back. THIS IS MY FINAL DECISION! -Willie McMiller."

My mouth dropped. I told Sean this was my girlfriend who didn't want me on the show. When I asked her about the email, she told me that I had to choose between her and *College Hill*. Before we met the cast, I was in the hotel the day before. One of the EPs came to me and told me that they cast me because I was funny. They had it down to a science!

I enrolled in four classes. I excelled in college and found out that I'm not dumb. I simply learned differently, and I went to a pretty much an all-white high school. This exposure to the culture was amazing! I ended up meeting lifelong friends and family. I took an African and Caribbean History class, and I learned so much of our culture. My conversations changed. My knowledge changed. My eyes were opened, and I realized we were amazing! The darker you are the sexier you are!

For the promotion for the show, I was asked to do a lot of radio interviews. Radio hosts would say, "Man, you are hilarious. Tell us a joke." People asked me that so many times that I wrote my first joke. I graduated with a B.A. in Marketing and the goofy, preacher's kid found his way because of *College Hill* and that HBCU experience.

About Willie Macc

Willie Macc (born Willie McMiller, August 4, 1984) has quickly come a long way as a member of young black Hollywood since first becoming known to a national television audience as the funny man on BET's extremely popular *College Hill: Virgin Islands*. He has become one of the few reality TV stars to make the transition from reality TV to that of a working actor in Hollywood.

In his season of *College Hill* (Season 4), four students from Los Angeles and four students from the Virgin Islands lived together while they were taking classes at The University of the Virgin Islands. Filled with the usual fun times, arguments and chaos that a house full of eight students normally bring, the living situation was pretty much business as usual for him since he had grown up in a relatively large household. The success of his season on *College Hill* allowed him to develop a huge following and name recognition among urban audiences between the ages of 15-34.

He has been quite busy since his "graduation" from *College Hill*. Once he relocated back to Los Angeles from the Virgin Islands, he continued his small screen run by appearing on multiple episodes of *CSI*, as well as *Journeyman*, Hulu's *Casual*, and TruTV's *Laff Mobb's Laff Track*, where he filmed one of his jokes that he wrote about earring skinny jeans. He has also appeared in several national and regional commercials, including Progressive, Verizon, Taco Bell, Pump Water, where he was the spokesperson of "Pump", a bottled water brand in New Zealand, and over forty more.

Willie Macc's big screen break came with his appearance in the comedy spoof "Meet the Spartans" where he played a "Yo Mama" joke, cracking opponent of the Spartan army. In his second film, *House Arrest*, Willie Macc co-stars as the Chris Tucker like sidekick in the *Friday* like home entertainment comedy. Cited as a "modern day Eddie Murphy," Willie Macc continues his destiny to stardom with two additional roles: being in the action/comedy, "Chicago Pulaski Jones" (written by and starring Kel Mitchel of the "Kenan & Kel" show, and includes a directorial debut by Cedric the Entertainer), and "The Greatest Song" (a wonderful romantic comedy starring Lamman Rucker of Tyler Perry's *Why Did I Get Married* and *Meet the Browns*, and national comedian and TV Host, Joe Clair).

In 2020, Willie sold his show *My Flipping Family* to HGTV, where he and his brother Jonathan bought and flipped homes around St. Louis from his personal proceeds. The brothers have been investing in properties since 2013 when they purchased a small, rundown home in Jennings for $7,000 in a tax lien sale. The house was in a state of major disrepair, with significant water damage and ceilings that were on the verge of caving in. In 2017, Jon was looking to leave his corporate accounting job at Boeing and began a career in real estate full-time. He turned to Willie who, by that time, was landing consistent acting jobs and making more money than at any other point in his career.

After Jon asked Willie, "What are you doing with all that money you've made in the entertainment industry?" Willie replied, "It's stacked up in the bank." Jon, seeing an opportunity, asked his brother, "Why don't you bring that money to St. Louis? Let's start acquiring properties."

Both an actor and comedian, Willie Macc made his first professional stand-up comedy debut at the famous BB Kings at Universal Walk in Los Angeles on July 31, 2007. He continues to hone his comedic skills by performing stand-up comedy routines in and around Los Angeles, and he can be regularly seen on the Laugh Factory and Comedy Store, but travels as a standup comedian.

Willie Macc has two podcasts called "Aye Old," which he does with his son. They have gathered over 500,000 followers on Instagram and TikTok. Willie's other podcast is AfroNoodles, which he does with his roadie and friend, Danny Plom. AfroNoodles is on tour doing standup across the U.S. and working on a pilot script to TV.

Willie Macc cites Bernie Mac, Martin Lawrence and Eddie Murphy as his role models. He spells his name with two Cs so it would not be too confusing with Bernie Mac. But like Bernie Mac, Willie Macc aspires to one day have his own TV show.

IDESHA FRASER
Friendliest

Redefining Cultural Norms
Idesha Fraser
Season 4

HBCUs have often been the cornerstone of communities and home to many of the finest minds in our society. I like to think that my HBCU journey was predestined. Years of hard work were finally paying off and I was granted a seat at our local university, The University of the Virgin Islands – the only HBCU outside the continental U.S. – at the end of my junior year of high school. As an early admission student, I had the privilege of experiencing some of the most rewarding times of my life while most of my friends were finishing their senior years. My first positive HBCU experience was the sense of community and camaraderie that I felt as soon as I stepped foot on campus. From the first moment, it seemed like everyone genuinely wanted to get to know each other and create strong relationships. The faculty and staff were also incredibly invested in helping us succeed and providing the resources we needed to do so. I was always able to find a place to call home in the dorms, and the friendliness of the RAs and other students was always a welcome sight. Additionally, the clubs and organizations on campus provided a wonderful way to meet new people and find a place to fit in.

The friendships I have made during my time at my HBCU were authentic and long-lasting. By my second year at UVI, I had found my people, that group of friends that are more like family, the ones you share *everything* with. It is these relationships that I cherish the most when I reflect on my time at my HBCU, and it is the confidence I built from having such a dynamic village that led me to try out for *College Hill* when auditions were held that fall so long ago.

During the summer of 2006, BET executives came to scout the campus. As luck would have it, I was working on campus for the Student Housing department that summer and heard about *College Hill* for the first time after speaking with them. That very night, I hopped online and found clippings of a prior season. While it looked like tons of fun, there was no way that I would ever be a part of a reality show. I packed the information away and as the months passed, forgot all about the show. Fall came and UVI was buzzing with new and returning students, excitement, and energy. The BET executives, with a huge entourage, also returned. It was time for auditions.

I remember purposely staying far away as possible during Day 1 of auditions. Reality TV?? Nope! Not doing it. Day 2 came along and some of my friends wanted to "just see" what was going on, so we all walked down the infamous UVI hill and headed to the Sports & Fitness Center. We didn't get in line, instead, we found a small table with a few chairs off to the side and sat there. We were having fun outside the casting room, talking to the people we knew who were waiting to audition, telling jokes, and honestly, being quite loud. This man walked up to the table, sat down, and easily joined the conversation. None of us knew who he was but we kept on chatting and laughing and interacting with all the other students nearby. After some time, this unknown man encouraged us to audition and, so we could say we did it, we all waited for the line to disappear and then joined the last wave of students entering the casting room.

Finding out I was selected to join the cast was the biggest OH SHIT moment of my life. I am not an "in front of the camera" type of girl. I value my privacy and enjoy doing what I want when I want to. Deciding to accept the offer was probably the least Idesha-like thing to do at that time, but I did it. When would I ever get another opportunity like this?? I packed up my dorm room and headed to the house. Boy oh boy, what a time!

I don't need to go into detail about our time in the house. You all saw what happened (albeit heavily edited, not chronological, and sometimes highly instigated by the production team version). Overall, my time on *College Hill* was an overwhelmingly positive one. From the connections I have made to the experiences we had as a cast, I was incredibly fortunate to have been part of such a unique and impactful show. Working through all the conflict, and being forced to deal with real-life trauma, all helped shape me into the person I am today. Facing adversity is important because it builds resilience, encourages critical thinking skills, and teaches us how to cope with demanding situations. It can be a wonderful opportunity for personal growth, helps us develop a more realistic view of the world, and teaches us valuable lessons about how to manage challenging circumstances.

Today, I work in project management for one of The Big Four. In an environment created for and designed by men, being strong-willed is a good thing! Being strong-willed has helped me thrive in corporate America by allowing me to stay focused on my goals while also pushing me to take risks and take on challenges that I may not have otherwise. It has given me the confidence to speak up when I have ideas or when I see room for improvement, and it has helped me stay resilient in the face of opposition or resistance. Additionally, being strong-willed has enabled me to stay organized and on-task, thereby allowing me to make the most of my efforts and achieve greater success.

Our season was not all roses and rainbows, but I hope it told the true story of human interaction and engagement, and the huge role cultural norms play in day-to-day life. I hope that our story helps to inspire and motivate people to think differently about cultures unlike their own, and to find ways to be more inclusive and equitable. By looking at how cultures interact, we can learn to respect and appreciate the unique values and beliefs of each individual and community.

About Idesha Fraser

Idesha Fraser is an alum of the University of the Virgin Islands and holds a master's degree in public health. Based in New York City, she has over fourteen years of professional experience in strategy, operations and project management. In her current role, Idesha is responsible for developing and executing strategies to achieve business objectives. She is also responsible for managing her team's operations and ensuring compliance with company policies.

Idesha is a wife, mom of two, and altruist throughout her local community. When not climbing the ladder of corporate America, she spends her time serving as co-president for her local school PTA and sits on the executive board of the district Presidents' Council. Idesha is passionate about empowering the next generation of leaders and is an active mentor to high school students in the NYC area. She strives to help her mentees recognize their potential and encourages them to achieve their goals. Through her work, she hopes to create a more equitable and just society. Idesha is an avid reader, a binger of true-crime shows, and 100% an island girl.

Never Stop Learning & Look Good While Doing It!
Kasheef Wyzard
Intern

As the first of four children born to parents of Caribbean descent, two guiding principles were instilled in me: never stop learning and look good while doing it!

As a participant in a school busing program called METCO in the city of Boston, I learned early that education could take me places. I got up every day at 5:30 a.m. in order to ride a special bus that took inner city kids over an hour out to suburban schools. There were occasional social challenges being one of the few Black kids in a mostly white school. But overall, I thrived as a student.

Eventually, the challenges of inner-city Boston drove my parents to relocate our family to Georgia. This move caused an immediate shift in my life. I was in high school now. No longer was I one of the few Black kids in school. Metro-Atlanta and surrounding counties gave me immediate exposure to people of color making moves! Black colleges, a Black mayor, and Black-owned businesses were things I never saw, nor imagined, growing up in Boston! I love the city that raised me, but Georgia afforded me access to more! Two years of high school in Georgia ultimately influenced my decision to stay in Atlanta for college versus hooping at a small-town college, or even leaving the state.

Several Atlanta universities were on my radar, including Georgia State University, Morehouse, Clark Atlanta University, and Georgia Tech. These are all great schools that have produced many successful alumni. My final choice came down to one factor: scholarship and tuition. With Georgia's Hope Scholarship in-hand, I decided to attend Georgia State University.

I know you're thinking, "Wait … that's not an HBCU. Is it?" To answer your question, no it is not. However, if there was ever an institution deserving of an honorary HBCU pass, it's Georgia State University! Not only does it look and feel like an HBCU when you're on the yard on a Tuesday or Thursday at 12:15 p.m., but, statistically, no other college moves more Black people into higher economic potential. Let me state it clearly… Georgia State University graduates more Black people than any college in the nation. It is officially classified as a minority-serving institution: 41% of the student body is Black, 15% is Asian and 12% is Hispanic. Side note: The ratio of male to females attending the school may or may not have been the cherry on top!

If Boston raised me, Georgia State University certainly made me. At this time, I'm officially fending for myself, surrounded by majority Black and brown young adults with high hopes and unabashed freedom. What a time to be alive! When I think back on it, there's no other chapter in my life where I had this much *access* and *freedom*.

Georgia State University gave me access to people and resources that I'd benefit from nearly fifteen years later! These are folk who have been in my wedding, been appointed as godparents to my son, and people who have opened doors to my professional career and more.

As stated, I had the space and freedom to figure it out at Georgia State University. There were times where I just didn't have "it." I failed a class, or I was broke and had to pool resources with my friends to make spaghetti. If you know, you know. These are the same people who also helped me realize I had "it" simultaneously, leading to other doors opening up.

I knew nothing of fraternities or sororities when I got to school. As mentioned earlier, I'm a first-generation American to parents of Caribbean descent. I had no exposure to Greek life before school, so they all were the same to me. My initial perception was that they hopped around and/or chanted for attention. I was prejudiced. I'd think to myself, "I don't need *none* of that to pull no girls." It was always in me, never on me. My initial assumptions about fraternities and sororities were definitely misinformed, though. Not all fraternities and sororities were present on the yard. I knew little of their missions and purposes.

Halfway through the first semester of my sophomore year, I learned of Kappa Alpha Psi Fraternity, Incorporated. This organization had a distinctive look and feel to it. Frankly, something felt familiar. There I was, actually humbling myself to consider being a part of something bigger. The more research I did, and the more brothers I met, the more real it got for me, "I think I found where I belong!" No one prepared me for what ensued next. A bond with nine other young Black men was fortified, and I crossed as a member of Kappa Alpha Psi Fraternity, Inc. in the fall of 2004. I ascended into the role of Polemarch (or president) of the Kappa Theta Chapter and was appointed into a regional position representing the Southeastern Province. The city had minimal active chapters of Kappa Alpha Psi on the yard, *plus* Facebook had just launched. Things got crazy! We brought back a "sexy/cool" that the city was missing! People traveled from across the country to attend our events—pajama parties included! Our swag was undeniable. Our shoulders were uncontrollable. The city was ours!

My presence on the yard and in the city crossed over to Facebook and Myspace. I used these platforms to promote parties and other activations. If you want to hear a testimony about my parties yourself, go to YouTube and search *"This is the Story of the Greatest Party That Never Happened"* by Dormtainment.

It was around this time that a casting agent for *College Hill* messaged me and said, "Tomorrow is the last day for casting in Atlanta. We'd love to meet you if you are interested." Reality TV was taking over at the time, and nothing was a bigger buzz than *College Hill*. I never aspired to be on television but understood this was a unique opportunity. I went to the casting call and interviewed, telling personal stories and being authentically me. I left the meeting unsure, but thankful for the unique interview experience. Months later, I received a call from a 323-area code that would change my life. History would soon be made!

The call from BET didn't feel real. Once the offer was extended to join the cast of *College Hill: Interns* in Chicago, I jumped on it. I wanted to have a unique experience, go to a new city, and put on for my people being authentically me!

Oftentimes, you don't realize what you're a part of when you're in it. That was my filming experience! Here I am again, experiencing a formative moment in my life with nine other strangers, fortifying bonds with my cast members that would echo through American television history. My college experience prepared me for this!

Because my season *College Hill: Interns* had a professional and competitive spin, I was able to put the experience on my resume. I described working for a major communications firm because of the various ad campaigns we worked on while on the show! This means that my college diploma and *College Hill: Interns* experience both directly influenced me getting my first job out of college!

Fast forward fifteen years later, and I'm fortunate to say that I'm doing all the things I was called to do! I understand that we are all the literal *sum* of our experiences. My experiences helped me see the world from vantages and disadvantages, helping me hone my superpower: empathy! In my current role as a leader in tech equity spaces, health and wellness, husband and a dad, I'm able to build and propose solutions that move my people from the inside out. I don't take any of the work for granted. I'm working in my purpose!

If there's something to take away from my story, I'd say it's this: *"You don't know how your story will end. Each moment or chapter builds on the next! Take advantage of as many opportunities and unique life experiences as you're able to. This will give depth and broaden your understanding as to how you see and can influence the world!"*

Never stop learning and look good while doing it!

About Kasheef Wyzard

As a first-generation American born to parents of Caribbean descent, Kasheef attributes the alignment of his career and purpose to interventions and exposure to educational resources far outside of the community that raised him. With such a dichotomy between the two worlds he grew to know, an unshakeable commitment to empower people within his community and other underrepresented groups was born.

Attending Georgia State University was one of the critical stops along his journey. Surrounded by young, Black excellence, Kasheef realized his leadership capabilities, propelling him to become a member of Kappa Alpha Psi Fraternity, Incorporated, where he served as the Chapter President. Doors continued to open as Kasheef grew in confidence to be his authentic self, eventually landing him a spot on the historic *College Hill* reality TV series. What a time to be alive!

Over ten years later, Kasheef has ascended in his career, excelling in business development, partner development, and programming. For the last six years, he's helped organizations move diversity and inclusion strategies forward, aligning corporations and community needs with unique programmatic opportunities.

To date, Kasheef is the National Director of Dream.Org's tech program, which leverages technology to attain transformative change in Black and brown communities by creating better access to technical careers and entrepreneurial capital for diverse leaders. Additionally, Kasheef owns a personal training facility in Metro-Atlanta, called "Put Up Resultz" where he collaborates with individuals and organizations of all kinds to create a healthier future! Kasheef is a proud husband and father of one!

ANTHONY ADIGHIBE
Most Likely to Become a Successful Entrepreneur

School Daze
Anthony Adighibe
Season 5

My college experience took place on the campus of Clark Atlanta University, also known as CAU. My journey before being accepted started as a transfer from Delaware State University, along with Essex County Community College in New Jersey. Before I was finally able to get into CAU, I had to do a year at Atlanta Metro Community College. Needless to say, I've been through tumultuous times, but I finally landed at CAU. My friends would be surprised to know that my first choice was to run track at Morehouse College. But that didn't work in my favor. It may have been the best backup decision I've gone with in my life that I'm grateful to have experienced.

I grew up loving the TV show *A Different World* and the movie *School Daze*, like I'm sure most Black adults in my age group did. So, it was always on my mind to experience this culture firsthand. Clark Atlanta didn't disappoint. What made this experience even doper was knowing that there are three neighboring schools: Spelman, Morehouse and Morris Brown, that were literally five minutes walking distance if you were walking from the famous Promenade, best known as The Strip. It was always a vibe kicking it in between classes on The Strip. I believe when I attended, the ratio of women to men was 8 to 1. So, it was all smiles for me every day.

After settling in with my classes and living arrangement, I was able to focus on campus activities in which I formed a promotion company with my close friends called HittSquad Entertainment. We quickly beat out the fraternities and sororities when it came to throwing the best parties on campus and in the city. We left such a great mark on the campus that seventeen years after our first start date, we are still able to do the biggest homecoming events for well over 3000 alums. Now it wasn't always parties for us. We were good at fundraising and even producing scholarship checks for numerous years for incoming freshmen.

The greatest thing about my journey in the first few years is me witnessing firsthand the transition of Atlanta turning into Black Hollywood. Although it was quite common to see stars/celebrities on The Strip, or performing at our student center, just imagine being a student literally from a random state and not being used to seeing or having access to notable faces. It was sort of a shell-shocking experience.

It was the end of spring semester in 2008. My friends and I heard about auditions for some college reality TV show that I'd never watched called *College Hill*. My friend convinced me to go, but unfortunately, none of us were selected at the time. Fast forward to fall semester of 2008. My good friend and business partner Korey Felder reached out to me and said, "Hey, bro! They are looking for someone just like you for this show."

I said, "What do you mean just like me?"

He said, "You know the man on campus, pretty boy type."

I laughed and said, "I'm good." After some convincing, I ended up going to the interview. I was the very last cast member selected for the *College Hill Atlanta edition*. Little did I know, life was about to change for me. I'm assuming because of the negativity the show might've received in years past, our universities didn't allow access to tapes on campus. That didn't matter because the word had spread across all campuses that myself along with Shavon (CAU), Dorion (CAU), and Dennis (Morehouse) had been selected. So of course, the red carpet was out everywhere we went.

I met everyone for the first time on our bus. I was at least two to four years older than everyone. So, my stance on everything was to try not to embarrass myself, but instead, use this time to brand myself and my promotion company. The producers definitely hated that I wore promo shirts in every interview. I used most of my time in the first few days to learn about people. The mini mansion we lived in was dope. We had access to a jacuzzi and a bar in the backyard. So, I definitely had to make sure we threw a party there, but even that got out of hand. My fondest memory was when I had my brother Mike Bradshaw arrange for some exotic dancers to come to the house so I could help introduce the world to Atlanta strip clubs. One could say I was extremely intentional in providing all sorts of entertainment.

There were times when I really felt like most of the cast didn't like each other and were extremely fake. I remained neutral. Entertainment wise, all of my castmates brought something to the table. It was a beautiful thing to watch it unfold. I had great talks with Dorion and Dennis separately about goals and dreams beyond this experience. To see their dreams manifest is a proud big brother moment. I always told them that, one day, I would own a club. Years later, I made that happen with the opening of Oak Atlanta in 2018.

Nowadays when you watch reality TV shows, you see a lot of fake instances. I'm proud that 95% of what we taped was real. The 5% that was fabricated came from a real place of anger, but we were bored one time and made sure we escalated an argument stemming from us not getting in a club because of the girls not bringing their IDs. There were a lot of arguments/confrontations that were extremely real, which I found myself having to calm down or just stay completely out of it. I just didn't ever want to be that representation on TV that the public would view as a clown or extra. Maybe I was overthinking it because when I see our people on TV now, all I see is clout chasers and clowns getting paid, and I just shake my head.

The time we went overseas was a bittersweet experience. It was great to travel, but it was annoying because the U.K. in the winter is almost worse weather wise than New York in the winter. There were a lot of cultural differences, and I didn't care for the food. I did appreciate the club experience and the way the London women went crazy when they saw the cameras on us (just kidding).

The last few days in the mini mansion were intense. There were a lot of emotions knowing that this experience was almost over. So, it became a time where true feelings were put on the table because everyone was going in their own direction after. Anyone that signs up for an experience like this should first be able to live in a confined space with most people who are nothing like you. That's 75% of the battle. The other 25% are being comfortable being yourself in front of the camera. I genuinely enjoyed my time on the show as it helped me propel my endeavors in the nightlife industry. Much love to all of my castmates: Dennis, Dru, Sira, Ash R., Ash L., Dorion and Shavon. We will forever be linked to each other. Special thanks to Chaka Zulu, Sean Rankine and Tracy Edmonds for the opportunity.

About Anthony Adighibe

Anthony Adighibe, who is of Liberia/Nigerian/Russian descent, was born in Brooklyn, New York and raised in South Orange, New Jersey. Before he relocated to Atlanta for college, in 2001, he was ranked second in the county, running a 6.42 at the 55-meter dash and fifth in the state at 10.82 in the 100-meter dash. His 100-meter record still stands at Columbia High School.

Before television fame on BET's *College Hill*, he attended Clark Atlanta University, majoring in Mass Media Arts. Over the last 16 years, Anthony has made quite the name for himself as one of Atlanta's premiere nightlife entrepreneurs. His list of accomplishments and his company, Hittsquad Ent, was voted promoter of the year at the Igrushi Awards show.

From 2018 to 2021, he was the owner of Oak Atlanta night club, which garnered attention all over the West Coast and southeast from celebrity appearances from Diddy, 50 Cent, Kevin Hart, Cardi B, Lil Baby, Jermaine Dupri, Money Bagg Yo, Omari Hardwick, and Future, to name a few.

Easily one of the hardest working men in Atlanta, Anthony also works with Gravity Multimedia Group, catering to marketing, events and promotions. He is currently partner at Westside Cultural Arts Center and co-owner of Tulum Restaurant in Atlanta.

TIFFANY GRAVES
Most Likely to Wear 20 Pearls

One Decision Can Change Your Life
Tiffany Graves
Season 6

Where do I begin? I should give some backstory to understand why my HBCU experience meant so much to me. Growing up in Trenton, New Jersey, there were few options for high schools. The first and only public option is Trenton High, which has now been renovated. It was falling apart and overcrowded back then. The other option is where I went to school: Trenton Catholic Academy. It's a small, private Catholic school. We had to wear uniforms and pay yearly tuition. In my graduating class, there were maybe sixty-four students. High school wasn't my favorite part of my time in New Jersey. Thankfully, everything wasn't all bad there. I met a guidance counselor named Ms. Smith my junior year. She was one of the very few teachers/staff that looked like me. She taught me what an HBCU was, their value, and why she thought it was important for me to explore that as an option. She had a poster on her wall with every HBCU in the United States, and I knew I wanted to go to one in Florida. After making that decision, everything else just fell into place.

I was excited to explore the different options in the state. With some guidance, I decided to attend Florida Memorial University in Miami, Florida. It's a smaller private college that gave me more one-on-one classroom experience and had a tighter community base to support its students. I knew transitioning from Trenton and high school wouldn't be easy, but finding a school that provided this type of environment definitely helped with that. I had to get used to seeing students, professors and staff that look like me. Don't get me wrong; there were Black people in my high school. But it was nothing like my HBCU experience. I always felt a sense of inclusion, like I belonged.

One of the first things I learned about Florida Memorial University is that we have Lion Pride and call our school FMU, or FLOMO, for short. Some of my favorite things to do there were dancing in front of Robinson Hall, being on the cheerleading team, going to the cafe to eat and hang out, or hanging out by the lagoon. Being able to be in such a comfortable atmosphere meant everything to me. Now, add being able to participate in the first Black college reality show to the mix and try to take in my sense of gratefulness and gratitude to God for the opportunity. Few people can say they went to an HBCU or were on the first-ever Black college experience reality TV show. I can, and that's so dope to me. I'm beyond blessed to have experienced both.

I got a message on Facebook, asking if I would be interested in doing the show and if I was willing to fill out an application. I felt special because I didn't go to the casting for it, but I was also nervous that I would get my hopes up and be let down. To my surprise, I got a phone call asking me to do an interview. Before I knew it, I was doing a physical and psych exam. It all felt like it happened so fast. It was hard for me to digest what was happening. Before I knew it, a camera crew was in my apartment with production, who then took me to where I would meet up with the rest of my roommates.

Living in the *College Hill* house was challenging for me for many reasons, one of which was being recorded all the time. I should've known what I was signing up for, but I don't think I did. I wasn't ready for that life. You could tell as you watch the season that I was quiet and timid, which is not me at all. Another challenge was living with such big and different personalities. My roommates were amazing. They were all from different schools and different walks of life, but they could definitely be a lot sometimes. On the flip side, my roommates were also the reason for a lot of great memories in that South Beach mansion.

There were many jokes, laughs, hugs and cuddles for the books. Is it weird that some of my favorite moments were trying to figure out what we were going to eat or where we were going out that night? We also did a lot of community service. It was one of my favorite parts of the journey. From going to a community center to helping a woman and her kids have a place to live and rebuild, those are the things that matter most in life and help build our legacy as human beings to leave a mark on this world. I'm not really sure why I did *College Hill*. Being on TV wasn't on my bucket list until it was presented to me. But if I had to answer the question now as to why I did the show, it would definitely be because, not only did I get to meet such a dope and amazing group of people, but I got to do some really wonderful things for a community to which I was so new. Living in the house helped me meet people and learn about them and my surroundings.

After *College Hill*, I returned to my normal day-to-day life as a student. I became a member of the illustrious Alpha Kappa Alpha Sorority, Incorporated. Greek life at FMU is excessively big. I knew that I wanted to be an AKA. Watching them stroll and step on the yard was unlike anything I had ever seen. That was another reason I didn't fully open up while filming. I always had the thought of them watching me in the back of my mind. I didn't want to disappoint! Needless to say, it was a great decision and worked out for the best.

I graduated FMU with a Bachelor of Science in biology and decided to take a year off. To make some money after graduation, I started modeling and doing music videos, which helped me network and meet a lot of different people. As my year off ended, I thought I wanted to be a dentist. So, I started my process to apply to schools. While shadowing a few different dentists as a prerequisite for school, I realized it wasn't what I wanted to do. Instead, I started working for one of them while I figured out my next step.

I realized later that my passion was traveling and living a more relaxed, slow-paced lifestyle. What I discovered mattered most to me this entire time was my happiness. Like any of us, I've had days where I wasn't so happy, of course. But, for the most part, I've lived a great life in my thirty-four years filled with happiness, great memories, many blessings, travels, once-in-a-lifetime experiences, and joy. I hope someone reading this sees that it takes one decision and one move for you to change your entire life for the better. I don't know if I would have been able to have a lot of my experiences if it wasn't for me making the decision to relocate to Florida for school. If you're considering attending an HBCU, or joining a sorority or fraternity, do it! Being Black is not only a thing of beauty; it's magic. Live your life and be happy. Don't just exist in the moment, hoping that one day you will truly feel alive. Be exceptional!

About Tiffany Graves

Tiffany Graves is a native of Trenton, New Jersey, and she resides in South Florida. She has a Bachelor of Science in Biology from Florida Memorial University. Her love for science matches her passion for cooking, traveling and discovering new cultures. Tiffany is an avid foodie, an animal lover, and a skilled photographer who traded in her modeling career to get behind the camera. She enjoys capturing special moments and creating memories through her photographs. Tiffany can't resist a good donut and she is always looking for the next great culinary experience. After completing her college education, Tiffany embarked on a journey to explore various countries, with her ultimate dream being to visit every continent. Her life motto is to live every day to the fullest because merely existing should never be an option.

America's First Black Reality TV Series Trivia

Home of the Jaguars, which HBCU was *College Hill* Season 1 filmed at?
A: SOUTHERN UNIVERSITY

Home of the Lions, which HBCU was *College Hill* Season 2 filmed at?
A: LANGSTON UNIVERSITY

Home of the Trojans, which HBCU was *College Hill* Season 3 filmed at?
A: VIRGINIA STATE UNIVERSITY

Filmed in St. Thomas, which HBCU did the *College Hill* Season 4 cast attend for classes?
A: UNIVERSITY OF THE VIRGIN ISLANDS

On the spin-off series INTERNS filmed in Chicago, which HBCU was represented in the cast?
A: NORTH CAROLINA A&T

Filmed in Atlanta, which three (3) HBCUs were represented in the cast for Season 5?
A: MOREHOUSE COLLEGE, CLARK ATLANTA UNIVERSITY and SAVANNAH STATE UNIVERSITY

Filmed in South Beach, which two (2) HBCUs were represented in the cast for Season 6?
A: FLORIDA MEMORIAL UNIVERSITY and FLORIDA A&M UNIVERSITY

Home of the Tigers, which HBCU was *College Hill Celebrity Edition* Season 1 filmed at?
A: TEXAS SOUTHERN UNIVERSITY

Which HBCU did Celebrity Edition 1 cast member Nene Leakes, originally enroll and attend briefly?
A: MORRIS BROWN COLLEGE

Home of the Hornets, which HBCU was *College Hill Celebrity Edition* Season 2 filmed at?
A: ALABAMA STATE UNIVERSITY

Which HBCU did Celebrity Edition 1 & 2 cast member Ray J, originally enroll and attend briefly?
A: PHILANDER SMITH COLLEGE

Which historically black collegiate fraternities are featured within the *College Hill* alumni?
A: ALPHA PHI ALPHA FRATERNITY INC. (Gabriel), KAPPA ALPHA PSI FRATERNITY INC. (Kasheef), OMEGA PSI PHI FRATERNITY INC. (Delano, Arlando) and PHI BETA SIGMA FRATERNITY INC. (Rodney)

Which historically black collegiate sororities are featured within the *College Hill* alumni?
A: ALPHA KAPPA ALPHA SORORITY INC. (Tiffany G.) and DELTA SIGMA THETA SORORITY INC. (Veronica)

Which two cast members were both HBCU mascots featured in the opening for their *College Hill* season?
A: Ray Cunningham (Season 3 Virginia State University) and Ray J (Celebrity Edition Season 2 Alabama State University)

According to RP Podcast
CEO/Founder: Ritha Pierre, Esq.
@accordingtorp
accordingtorp@gmail.com

AC Events
The Luxury Planning Experience
CEO/Founder: Amy Agbottah
amy@amycynthiaevents.com

ACTIVate
CEO/Founder: Yladera Drummond, J.D.
contact@activateleadership.org
info@yladeradrummond.com
www.yladeradrummond.com
www.activateleadership.org

AD Bonner Music
CEO/Founder: Adrain Bonner
817-300-3995
adbonnermusic@gmail.com

Allen Financial Solutions
CEO/Founder: Jay Allen
@jay83allen
@Jay Allen
allen.jonathan83@gmail.com

AG Management & Business Consulting
CEO/Founder: Gabriel Langley
www.agmbc.com

The Alli Group, LLC
Real Estate Management
Founders: Lawrence & Nickia Alli
@thealligroupllc
nickia.alli@gmail.com
www.thealligroupllc.com

Alexander G. Events
CEO/Founder: Nathan Alexander Kemp
Nathan A. Kemp, 336-706-1422
Brooke G. Kemp, 336-944-4768
alexgevents20@gmail.com

AMMEA
President: Ernest Stackhouse
ej.stackhouse@gmail.com
www.ammea.org

The Ancestor Key
CEO/Founder: Ja'el Gordon
504-356-1466
theancestor@gmail.com

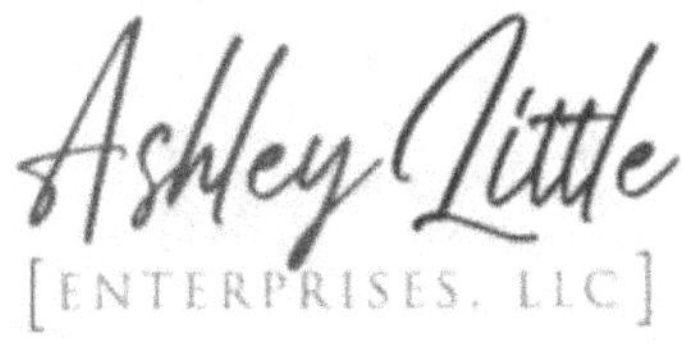

Ashley Little Enterprises, LLC
CEO/Founder: Dr. Ashley Little
@_ashleyalittle
@Ashley Little
aalittle08@gmail.com
www.ashleylittleenterprises.com

The Self-care Doc
CEO/Founder:
Dr. Raushannah Johnson-Verwayne
Licensed Clinical Psychologist &
Wellness Coach
@Ask Dr RJ
@Ask Dr RJ
www.AskDrRJ.com

Assurance Tax & Accounting Group, LLC
CEO/Founder:
Kimberlee Collins-Walker
8676 Goodwood Blvd., Ste. 102
Baton Rouge, LA 70876
225-757-7518
kim@assurancetaxbr.com
www.assurancetaxbr.com

Baker & Baker Realty, LLC
CEO/Founder: Christopher Baker
@seedougieblake
@Christopher D. Baker
baker.christopher@gmail.com

Balance Candle Bar
CEO/Founder: Lacey B. Evans
www.shopbalanceco.com

BLKWOMENHUSTLE

CEO/Founder: Lashawn Dreher

@blkwomenhustle

@Blk Women Hustle

info@blkwomenhustle.com

B G B
Bald Guys Bake

Bald Guys Bake, LLC

CEO/Founder: Torey Searcy

info@baldguysbake.com

www.baldguysbake.com

Beautiful Body & More, LLC

CEO/Founder: Melody Scott

318-716-1507

318-716-1508 fax

@Beautifulbodyandmore

@Beautiful Body & More, LLC

www.beautifulbodyandmore.com

Block Band Music & Publishing, LLC

CEO/Founder: D. Rashad Watters

919-698-2560

blockbandmusic@gmail.com

The Black Techies/Podcast

CEO/Founder: Herbert L. Seward, III

Where black culture meets the world of technology.

www.theblacktechies.com

Boardroom Brand, LLC

CEO/Founder: Samuel Brown, III

@_gxxdy

samuel.brown.three@gmail.com

Booked Cafe Books

CEO/Founder: Kierra Jones

@Booked Cafe Books

@Booked Cafe Books

contact@bookedcafebooks.com

www.bookedcafebooks.com

Bound By Conscious Concepts

CEO/Founder: Kathryn Lomax

@msklovibes223

@Klo-Kathryn Lomax

972-638-9823

klomax@bbconcepts.com

Brooks Art Collective

CEO/Founder: LaToya Brooks

@brooksartcollective

@brooksartcollective

brooksartcollective@gmail.com

BZAR STUDIOZ

CEO/Founder: Steven Baltazar

bzarstudioz@gmail.com

www.bzarstudioz.com

Caleb T. Dunbar Photography

CEO/Founder: Caleb T. Dunbar

@calebtdunbarphotography

@Caleb T. Dunbar Photography

calebtdunbar@gmail.com

www.calebtdunbar.com

Campaign Engineers

CEO/Founder: Chris Smith

@csmithatl

csmithl911@gmail.com

Chef Batts

CEO/Founder: Keith Batts

@chefbatts

booking@chefbatts.com

Cici's Freelance Services

CEO/Founder:

Courtney "Cici" Walker, MPA

@cicisfreelanceservices

225-288-8216

cicisfreelanceservices@gmail.com

Color Wheel Therapy

CEO/Founder: Kiandra Daniels

469-251-2418

kiandra.daniels@colorwheeltherapy.com

www.colorwheeltherapy.com

Commit 2 Life Fitness

CEO/Founder: Joseph T. Shaw III

@commit2lifefitness

The Bitter Suite Podcast

Apple & Spotify

@thebittersuite2020

www.commit2life.com

Cjenk The Agency: Creative Concierge, LLC

CEO/Founder: Chasmin Jenkins

chasminjenkins@gmail.com

CreativeED Consulting, LLC

CEO/Founder: Dr. William J. Earvin

wjeconsulting@icloud.com

Cultural Resources

CEO/Founder:

Corey "Mr. Hanky" Dennard

@culturalresources

amrhankybeat@gmail.com

Daily Life Managements LLC

CEO/Founder:

Kristy Lashaun Burrell

504-390-9949

Curves & Gains

CEO/Founder: Patrice Murphy

@curvesandgaines

curvesandgains@gmail.com

www.curvesandgains.com

DD Jones Enterprise

CEO/Founder: Darcele Jones-Horton

darceleh@bellsouth.net

Da Edge 1 Productions

CEO/Founder: Garrett Edgerson

@daedge1pro

www.daedge1pro.com

DDL Entertainment

CEO/Founder: Darryl Lassister

darryldlassiter@msn.com

Dee Ree Hair Co

CEO/Founder: Desiree R. Dawson

✉ desireeshanecedawson@yahoo.com

Deroune Services, LLC

CEO/Founder: Marina Zeno

📱 337-418-0785

Dr. Ashanti Says, LLC

CEO/Founder: Dr. Ashantia Says

🌐 www.drashantisays.com

🌐 https://linktr.ee/drashantisays

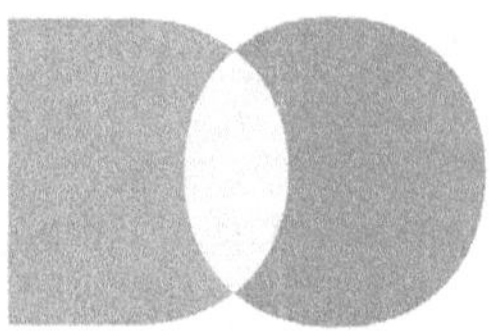

Dream.Org

CEO/Founder: Kasheef Wyzard

📷 @Dream.corps

🌐 www.dream.org

DS National Logistics

CEO/Founder: D. Scott

✉ Scottie.d1911@gmail.com

Dorian Troy Studios

CEO/Founder: Dorian Davis

✉ dorian@doriantroystudios.com

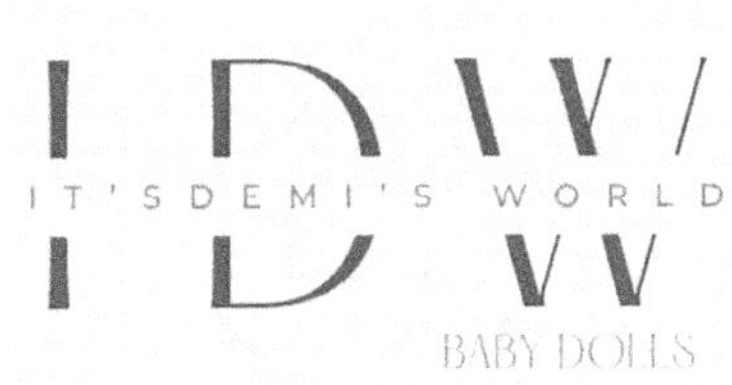

It's Demi's World Baby Dolls

CEO/Founder: Demi Scott

www www.itsdemisworld.com

Eclectikread Marketing

CEO/Founder: Christa Newkirk

@chris_ta_da

info@eclectikread.com

Elementz4 Designs, LLC

CEO/Founder: Gretta Frierson

www www.elementz4designs.com

www.linktr.ee/elementz4

engHERneered

engHERneered

CEO/Founder: Christina Caldwell, PE

engherneered@gmail.com

Enlightened Visions, Inc.

CEO/Founder: TaNisha Fordham

tanisha.fordham@gmail.com

www www.enlightenedvisions.org

Executive Reign

CEO/Founder: Canisha Cierra Turner

@Executive Reign

804-605-6875

www www.executivereign.com

www www.canishacierraturner.com

February First

CEO/Founder: Cedric Livingston

Director/Writer: *February First: A Stride Towards Freedom*

www www.februaryfirstmovie.com

Freeda's World Podcast
CEO/Founder: Ritha Pierre, Esq.
@freedas_world
accordingtorp@gmail.com

DJ General Mealz
CEO/Founder: Deitrich Armstrong
dtrickarmstrong@gmail.com

Give Black App
Co-Founder/COO: Alexus Hall
@giveblackapp
@Give Black App
@giveblackapp
www.giveblackapp.com

Happy Hour Investors
Co-Founder/Managing Partner:
   Jonathan Rivers
830 Glenwood Ave., Ste. 510-352
Atlanta, GA 30316
404-860-2288
jonathan@hhinvestors.com
www.hhinvestors.com

Harbor Institute
CEO/Founder:
   Rasheed Ali Cromwell, J.D.
@theharborinstitute
@The Harbor Institute
@harborinstitute
racromwell@theharborinstitute.com

Harvey Wilder-Foundation
CEO/Founder: Jordan Harvey
www.hawilfoundation.org

HBCU 101
CEO/Founder: Jahliel Thurman
@HBCU101
jahlielthurman@gmail.com
www.hbcu101.com

HBCU Cheer Black Excellence
@HBCUcheer
HBCUcheerleaders@yahoo.com

The HBCU Band Experience with Christy Walker
CEO/Founder: Dr. Christy Walker
christywalker57@gmail.com
www.christywalker.com

The HBCU Experience Movement, LLC
CEO/Founder: Dr. Ashley Little
@_ashleyalittle
@DrAshley Little
thehbcuexperiencemovement@gmail.com
www.thehbcuexperiencemovement.com

HBCU Buzz
(HBCU Buzz | Taper, Inc. | Root Care Health)
CEO/Founder: Luke Lawal, Jr.
@lukelawal
@L & COMPANY
301-221-1719
lawal@lcompany.co

HBCU Girls Talk
CEO/Founder: TeeCee Camper
@HBCUgirlstalk
talkgirls@yahoo.com

HBCU Grad

CEO/Founder: Todd Finley

312-535-8511

www.hbcugraduates.com

HBCU-NBDOC

www.hbcu-nbdc.org

HBCU HUB App

connects students directly to HBCUs

CEO/Founder: Dr. Darrius Brooks

@hbcuhub

www.hbcuhub.us

HBCU Pride Nation

CEO/Founder: Travis Jackson

@HBCUpridenation

@HBCU Pride Nation

travispjackson@gmail.com

HBCU Legacy Fashion

CEO/Founder: Cheylaina Fultz

@HBCULegacyFashion

@HBCULegacyFashion

contact@hbculegacyfashion.com

www.hbculegacyfashion.com

HBCU Pulse

CEO/Founder: Randall Barnes

@HBCUpulse

@thehbcupulse

www.hbcupulse.com

HBCU Recruitment Center

CEO/Founder:

Dr. Tomisha Brock-Price

3925 N. Martin Luther King Jr. Drive

Ste 209

North Las Vegas, NV 89032

✉ hbcurecruitmentcenter@gmail.com

🌐 www.hbcurecruitmentcenter.org

HBCU Times

CEO/Founders: David Staten, Ph. &
Bridget Hollis Staten, Ph.D

📷 @HBCU_times8892

📘 @HBCU Times

✉ hbcutimes@gmail.com

HBCU Wall Street

CEO/Founders:

Torrence Reed & Jamerus Peyton

📘 @HBCU Wall Street

✉ info@hbcuwallstreet.com

H.E.R. Story Podcast

H.E.R. Story with J. Jamison

CEO/Founder: Janea Jamison

📷 @herstory _podcast

#Herstorymovement

Hidden Colours

CEO/Founder: Jahlil Witt

✉ mr.jahlilwitt@gmail.com

Hitt Squad Ent

CEO/Founder: Anthony Adighibe

🌐 www.hittsquadent.com

Holistic Practitioners

CEO/Founder: Tianna Bynum

 @Tianna Bynum

 tpb33@georgetown.edu

The Hookah Bull, LLC

"An Elite Mobile Hookah Service"

Owner/Operator: Roy Ector II

 301-404-9735

 roy.ector@thehookahbull.com

 www.thehookahbull.com

ICG Marriage & Family Therapy

CEO/Founders:

 Jabari & Stephanie Walthour

 @thedopesextherapist

 stephanie@intimacycenterga.com

 www.intimacycenterga.com

iGive

CEO/Founder: Jessica Davis

 igiveglobal1@gmail.com

Johnson Capital

CEO/Founder: Marcus Johnson

 @marcusdiontej

 marcus@johnsoncap.com

Journee Enterprises

CEO/Founder: Fred Whit

 @frederickwjr

 @Fred Whit

 frederickwjr@yahoo.com

J.Robins CPA, LLC
CEO/Founder: Joseph Robins
@robinscpa
@jrobinscpa
9800 Line Hwy., Ste. 261
Baton Rouge, LA 70816
225-650-7306
info@jrobinscpa.com
www.jrobinscpa.com

The Lab Personal and Professional Development Center, LLC
CEO/Founder: Ebony Gourrier
www.thelabppd.com

Kelly Collaborative Medicine
CEO/Founder: Dr. Kathyrn Kelly
10801 Lockwood Dr., Ste. 160
Silver Spring, MD 20901
301-298-1040
www.kellymedicinemd.com

The Lady BUGS
CEO/Founder: Tatiana Tinsley Dorsey
@theladybugsoffical
@HBCU Times
ladybugs_HQ@googlegroups.com

K.Y. Turner Law Firm, PLLC
CEO/Founder: Khanay Turner, Esq.
khanay.turner@icloud.com

LEMM Media Group
CEO/Founder: Cremel Nakia Burney
@cremel_the_creator
cremelburney@gmail.com

Like Minds Dine Productions

CEO/Founder: Kristin J. Meyers

✉ tokristinmeyers@gmail.com

Little Publishing, LLC

CEO/Founder: Dr. Ashley Little

🅾 @_ashleyalittle

📘 @DrAshley Little

✉ info@ashleyalittle.com

🌐 www.ashleylittleenterprises.com

Swing Into Their Dreams Foundation

Co-Founders: Pamela Parker and
Lynn Demmons

✉ swingintotheirdreams@gmail.com

🌐 www.swingintotheirdreams.com

LK Productions

CEO/Founder: Larry King

🅾 @lk_rrproduction

📘 @Larry King

✉ lkproduction@yahoo.com

Lou's BluBooks

CEO/Founder: Louis D. Roberts

📠 202-560-7368

🌐 www.lousblubooks.com

Lynch Law, PLLC

CEO/Founder: Chance D. Lynch, Esq.
1015A Roanoke Ave., Ste. A
Roanoke Rapids, NC 27870

📠 252-535-1251

MaccBoyz Entertainment

CEO/Founder: Willie Macc

@WillieMacc

www.williemacc.com

Marching Sport

CEO/Founder: Gerard Howard

gerardhoward@gmail.com

The Marching Force

700 Emancipation Dr.

Hampton, VA 23668

www.supportthematchingforce.com

McKallen Medical

CEO/Founder: Sade Stephenson,
   MSN, RN, AGACNP-BC

9253 Hermosa Ave., Ste. B

Rancho Cucamonga, CA 91730

747-225-6776

mckallenmedical@gmail.com

www.mckallenmedicaltraining.com

The Marching Podcast

CEO/Founder: Joseph Beard

marchingpodcast@gmail.com

www.themarchingpodcast.com

Minority Cannabis Business Association

President: Shanita Penny

📘 @MCBA.Org

🐦 @MinCannBusAssoc

in @Minority Cannabis Business Association

📟 202-681-2889

✉ info@minoritycannabis.org

🌐 www.minoritycannabis.org

Mills Academy

CEO/Founder: Airneica Mills

📟 662-822-6976

✉ millsacademy1@gmail.com

MilRo Entertainment

CEO/Founder: Chevis Anderson

✉ milrosplace@yahoo.com

MMarie Event Planning & Logistics

CEO/Founder: Megan Clay

✉ meganmclay08@gmail.com

Mr. Anthony

CEO/Founder: Anthony Adighibe

✉ mr_anthony83@yahoo.com

Music GreekΣ, Inc.

CEO/Founder: Jeremiah Johnson

📟 470-615-9567

✉ musicgreeks@gmail.com

🌐 www.musicgreeks.com

NC Dance District

CEO/Founder: Dr. Kellye Worth Hall

@divadoc5

@Kellye Worth Hall

delta906@gmail.com

Never2Fly2Pray

CEO/Founder: Jeffrey Lee Sawyer

@never2fly2pray

@Jeffrey Lee

htdogwtr@yahoo.com

NXLevel Travel (NXLTRVL)

CEO: Hercules Conway

@herc3k

@Hercules Conway

COO: Newton Dennis

@nxlevel

@Newton Dennis

info@nxleveltravel.com

www.nxleveltravel.com

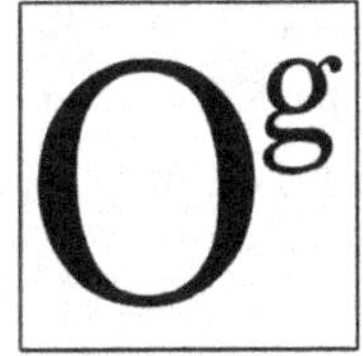

Original Garments: Clothing Brand

CEO/Founder: Dr. Darrius Brooks

@original.garments

Coming Soon (DM to purchase)

OEDM Group

CEO/Principal Owner: Justin Blake

@oedmgroup.com

contact@oedmgroup.com

www.oedmgroup.com

PacketStealer Gaming

CEO/Founder: David Matthews

✉ packetstealer@outlook.com

PILAR

Co-Owner: Nate Perry

⊙ @barpilar

✉ nate@pilardc.com

The Perfect Glow

CEO/Founder: Berrie Russell

✉ berrierussell@gmail.com

www www.tpglow.com

Props Enterprises, LLC

CEO/Founders: Clarence & Keyanda
Satchell

✉ foreversatchell@gmail.com

The Phoenix Professional Network

CEO/Founder: DJavon Alston

⊙ @thephoenixnetwork757

f @DJavon Alston

✉ thephoenixnetwork757@gmail.com

Put Up Resultz

CEO/Founder: Kasheef Wyzard

⊙ @PutUpResultz

www www.putupresultz.com

Queen Series
CEO/Founder: Randall Barnes
✉ aqueenseries@gmail.com

Raggedi Luxury Durags
CEO/Founder: Chasmin Jenkins
✉ chasminjenkins@gmail.com

Reach Higher
CEO/Founder: Dr. Kesha Reed
✉ info@keshareed.com

Reed Williams,
A Professional Law Corporation
CEO/Founder:
   Donald R. Williams, Jr., Esq.
9343 Tech Center Drive, Suite 165
Sacramento, CA 95826
☎ 916-281-9337
🌐 www.reedwilliamslaw.com

Regal PhotoBooth
CEO/Founder: Kaleena Clarkson
✉ kaleenajp@gmail.com

Reid Creative Solutions, LLC
CEO/Founder: Aja Reid
☎ 919-822-2892
✉ info@reidcreativesolutions.com
🌐 www.reidcreativesolutions.com

Rising Stars 3lite Cheer, Dance and Tumbling
CEO/Founders:
    Dr. Ke'Shawn Roberts and
    Ke'Shone Roberts
Central Texas
504-316-9325

SC DJ WORM 803
CEO/Founder: Jamie Brunson
@SCDJWORM803
@SC DJ Worm 803
@SCDJWORM803
@SC DJ Worm 803
scdjworm803@gmail.com
www.scdjworm803.com

Sassy Suga Lip Service
info@sassysuga.com
www.sassysuga.com

Seedlinks Behavior Management
CEO/Founder: Ryan L. Williams
1533 Marshall Street
Shreveport, LA 71101
318-626-5597

SayYes

Say Yes, LLC
CEO/Founder: Porscha Lee Taylor
@sayyesplanners
info@sayyescareer.com
www.sayyesplanners.com

Shani L., Relationship Enthusiast
CEO/Founder: Shani L.Farmer
@shanilrelationshipenthusiast
info@shanilfarmer.com
www.shanilfarmer.com

She Is Magazine

CEO/Founder: Ciara Horton

@sheisemagazine

@Ciara Horton

www.ciarasheisemagazine.com

Sneaux Bidness

CEO/Founder: Delano Holmes

@sneaux_bidnessla

Shonnie Murrell

BookShonnieMurrell@gmail.com

ShonnieMurrell@gmail.com

Special Occasion

CEO/Founder: Gary Norman II

@specialoccasionlive

www.specialoccasionlive.com

The Silent Majority

CEO/Founder: Rodney Henry

757-239-1039

www.dearsummerbbq.com

Social Status PR

CEO/Founder: Ray Cunningham

@SocialStatusPR

Southern University A&M College
801 Harding Blvd.
Baton Rouge, LA 70807
225-771-4500

Southern University Alumni Federation
124 Roosevelt Steptoe Dr.
Baton Rouge, LA 70807
225-771-4200
sualumni@sualumni.org

Springbreak Watches (SPGBK)
CEO/Founder: Kwame Molden
@SPGBK
@Kwame Molden
info@springbreakwatches.com

Stamp'd Travel
CEO/Founder:
Jocelyn Hadrick Alexander
@jocehadyou
jocelyn.h.alexander@gmail.com
www.stampdtravel.com

Strategic Consulting, LLC
CEO/Founder:
Desiree' C. Cotton-Turner, Esq.
4917 S. Sherwood Forest Blvd.
Baton Rouge, LA 70817
225-371-3638

Success and Religion
CEO/Founder: Micheal Taylor
successismyreligion@gmail.com

Sugar Top Spirit & Beverage Co.

CEO/Founder: Terri White

@sugartopspirits

@sugartopspirits

tl.white412@gmail.com

www.sugartopspirits.com

SwagHer

Vice President of Sales / Marketing:
Jarmel Roberson

@swaghermagazine

jroberson@swagher.net

www.swagher.net

TLW Photography

CEO/Founder: Taylor Whitehead

mrknowitall91@aol.com

Uplift Clothing Apparel

CEO/Founder: Jermaine Simpson

@upliftclothingapparel

www.upliftclothingapparel.com

Upward Path

CEO/Founder:
Cameron Chalmers Dupree

@upwardpathtc

contact@upwardpathtc.com

www.upwardpathtc.com

The Urban Learning & Leadership Center, Inc.

President/Co-Founder:
John W. Hodge, Ed.D

jhodge@ulleschools.com

Urban Millennial Lifestyle

CEO/Founder: Nolita R. Pore

@themonalita

@fitlikelita

contact@themonalita.com

www.themonalita.com

Vision Tree, LLC

CEO/Founder: Dr. Jorim Reed

@upwardpathtc

visiontreellc@gmail.com

The Vernon Group
Cooperative Solutions

CEO/Founder: Anthony V. Stevens

@investednu

info@vernongroupllc.com

Vision Unlimited, LLC

CEO/Founder: Kirby Denise Wilson

@Kirby_Denise_

@Kirby Denise

info@teamvisionunlimited.com

www.teamvisionunlimited.com

VJR Real Estate

CEO/Founder: Victor Collins, Jr.

@vjrtherealtor

vic@thevjrgroup.com

We Are Educated, Inc.

We Are Educated, Inc.

CEO/Founder: Ayanna Spivey

@ayannaceleste

ayanna.spivey@yahoo.com

Yardopoly

CEO/Founder: Ray Cunningham

@Yardopoly

yardopoly@gmail.com

www.thegamecrafter.com
(*search: Yardopoly*)

Yard Stubs

CEO/Founder: Cremel Burney

@YardStubs

partnerships@yardstubs.com

www.yardstubs.com

Zoom Technologies, LLC

CEO/Founder: Torrence Reed

@torrencereed3

support@zoom-technologies.co

Yard Talk 101

CEO/Founder: Jahliel Thurman

@YardTalk101

www.yardtalk101.com

www.ingramcontent.com/pod-product-compliance
Lightning Source LLC
Chambersburg PA
CBHW050346160726
48002CB00001B/477